LOVE

From Motion to Feeling

LOVE

from Motion to Feeling

A Memoir

JACK WIENER, LP, CDMT

IPBOOKS.net
International Psychoanalytic Books

International Psychoanalytic Books
New York • http://www.IPBooks.net

LOVE: from Motion to Feeling—A Memoir

Published by IPBooks, Queens, NY
Online at: www.IPBooks.net

Copyright © 2025 Jack Wiener

Manuscript editor: Carol L. Skolnick
Cover and book design: Noel S. Morado

ISBN: 978-1-956864-91-5

ACKNOWLEDGMENTS

To Aaron Thaler, PhD, psychologist, psychoanalyst, with whom during the early post-Covid sessions, the memoir *Love: From Motion to Feeling* was sparked.

To my wife, Arlette Thebault Wiener, who endured a relentless preoccupation with recapturing my past to its reasonable resting presence four years later.

To the late Lyn Pyle, teacher and student who contributed an insightful creative process for the dynamics of late adolescents. May she rest in peace.

And to the hundreds of children and adults who engendered pedagogic techniques over 60-plus years, giving rise to the essence of *grounded motion as feelings.*

CONTENTS

PREFACE

Feelings happen even though the heart is silenced, and the mind is voiceless.

In utero, before either feelings or voice flower, touch is our earliest sensation. It is a total body, mind, spirit *motion* of connection and safety.

This memoir is my journey of how this endowed sensory experience of touch—awakened consciously as a dance teacher over 60-plus years, and psychologically by my post Covid analytic therapy of terror—put me *in touch* with feelings. Through the lens of my present 90-year-old awareness, I comment on the sequence of events. I chose to begin with love.

I loved naturally without doubts. I lost love unforgivingly. I never thought about recovering love. Love's return was circuitous, filled with dismissive self-involvement, intellectual insights, and creative pedagogic explorations.

Regardless of whatever help I received, I was unconsciously on my own into my middle 80s. One sleepless night while recovering from Covid, an unbearable anxiety froze the fingertips of my right hand for a few terrifying seconds. It was followed by the image of sitting in a car as the driver at a STOP sign, totally confused whether to turn right or left. I was as close to paralysis as I had ever been.

As a long-practicing psychoanalyst at the time, I knew I needed help. Receiving it, began to melt my *"I know"* arrogance into the warming waters of gratitude. Feelings painfully, traumatically arose from their dormant lair.

The awakening professional explorations and insights began with an *inner shout*, in the spring of 1956, as I worried about what to believe in after discharge from Korea. *"I'm going to be an artist."* I was shocked and relieved.

Post discharge, I choreographed, danced, acted, directed theater, and founded a creative movement dance school that grew to 350 students from age three to adults, with an extensive curriculum and syllabus resulting in a first book, *Creative Movement for Children: A Dance Program for the Classroom* (1969), which achieved international recognition. I married, had two wonderful children, committed to years of psychanalytic therapy, graduated after 11 years of study and supervision as a certified practicing psychoanalyst to become a New York State licensed psychoanalyst.

In pursuit of self-awareness, I came to accept without shame dependency, humbly experiencing the *not knowing* experience of silence. Not knowingly, our body cells register everything, shaping our character...expressed in a smile, a kiss, an embrace, the lift of a spoon, the sound of our voice, the way we stand and walk.

Nerves pulse, muscles connect to bones, aligning, misaligning our *motion* without permission. Our body is a first responder to the evolutionary musculature registering, expressing emotions through habits, regardless of the mental skills we develop to deal rationally with life's urging and wishful insistences.

Using my body consciously—working my muscles throughout my adulthood, as well as through professional engagements and heightened hours of terror—I learned to tame the struggling, controlling mind and submit to uninvited feelings.

Developing my perceptual sensitivity to our innate capacity for the *continuity of motion* dovetailed skills, heart, and mind into the personal stories, professional revelations, practice, and emotional growth I share here with you.

IDEALS

In September of 1952, our group of 20-some from the U.S. and Canada members of Habonim, a Labor Zionist youth movement, arrived and settled into a relatively new kibbutz, Kfar Blum, in the northern part of Israel, the Galil. Kfar Blum was founded in 1943 by Habonim members from around the world, subsequently combined with a Latvian group that had to give up its kibbutz near the Dead Sea when the borders with Jordan were established by the United Nations in 1947.

Young, excited, dedicated idealists, we were looking forward to a nine-month immersion in daily, down to earth collective living: community breakfasts and dinners (lunch was usually at the worksites); farming, orchard tending, milking cows, raising chickens, harvesting fish from created ponds, the fruits of our labors to be sold commercially through a regional co-op. Our afternoons were taken up by Hebrew instruction and group activities. We attended Sunday meetings with the kibbutz members, discussing how to govern their economic responsibilities, housing needs, raising children, landscaping their environment, and meeting individual needs.

By June of '53, we all returned home from our adventure, wiser and more grounded regarding our idealistic aims. Some of our group would return to form their own collective community, or to settle into cities. Some might remain Zionist at heart, but would make other life choices.

1

During one late October group-gathering afternoon, we were asked by the sponsoring Jewish Agency for one interested volunteer to attend a leadership training program in Jerusalem, to fulfill a commitment for someone who because of illness was unable to go. Only two of us considered the request; the rest were committed to the collective experience. I was proud to be the one chosen. I left the kibbutz, and the group with which I came to Israel, knowing that I would return to Kfar Bloom for a three-month program before ending up back in Jerusalem for the termination of the leadership program.

It didn't cross my mind that I was abandoning friends. Friends I had grown up with through my teens. They were competitors, potential lovers, recipients of family bonds. It has taken me all of these years to recognize my unconsciously rationalized self-involvement. Was I fulfilling the socialist ideas and hopes of my parents? This assumption will become clearer as this journey unfolds.

I was excited by Jerusalem, the thousands of years-old center of Hebraic life, despite all the exiles and meanderings throughout the world. The kibbutz was interesting, and yet for me, it had the usual hierarchal dynamic of every other group: some individuals were more influential, others less involved. *A reflection on my unwitting isolated separate self, struggling with "What do I really want?"*

Staying there would also make it easier to be closer to my mother's younger sister Simah in Kholon, a small township just a short bus ride south of Tel Aviv. My aunt had migrated to Palestine in 1921, when it was still under the British mandate after World War I. I first saw her waving as our boat, the Negba, docked in Haifa. I was shocked by how much she looked like my mother. She exuded a happiness that was totally inviting, in contrast to her older sister. I looked forward to knowing her Jewish Iraqi husband and my Sabra (Israeli born), accordion playing cousin, slightly younger than me, aware but not as smitten by my pioneering kibbutz idealistic sentiments. My aunt Simah was the first relative I came to know and love as innocently as I loved my parents.

Why did I opt to separate from a group that was so much a part of my formative adolescent years? Was it my sense of adventure, modeled after my parents' migration from Warsaw to Cuba in the late 1920s? They were only 20 and 22 when they left. I can't recall them ever talking about how they felt about leaving Poland. I imagine my anxious mother, married, waiting excitedly to rejoin her love who had left three years earlier, and my papa relieved not to be drafted into the Polish Army, anticipating life on the warm Caribbean Island.

Imagining how they might have felt hints at how unconsciously, I had separated each parent to avoid their frightening conflicts. Was this my cerebrated way to accommodate my separate emotional self? A beguiling ownership, without any insight about what I was doing until I was in my 80s.

LOVE

Early winter of 1952-53. Within weeks of arriving at the training program in Jerusalem, her shiny red hair and her smile drew me in like the warming sun of early winter. We chatted, and chatted, and chatted, getting ever closer to a kiss. I began floating on the fizz, fizzing *motion* of love.

We spent the early part of many nights embracing quietly on her bed, as her roommate lay silently a few feet away. I couldn't get enough of her embraces and affectionate kisses. At a certain point, a signal of light announced that the building was soon to be shut for the night, the doors barred. I would quickly get out of her bed, run down the steps, and out of the building.

I walked by the light of the stars through an empty field to the men's building approximately a block and a half away. One time, a shout in Hebrew froze me: Israeli soldiers were stationed in the shadow dealing with incursions by West Bank Palestinians, crossing boundaries to steal. I stood motionless as I answered their questions, oblivious to fear, floating in the spell of *love motion*.

Amazing how fear can be blocked out by the embrace of a 19-year-old love. A self- encasing universe!

Not only was my Hebrew improving by leaps and bounds because of my Yiddish-speaking facility with Israeli intonations and inflections, but my prior schooling in grammar and conjugations placed me in classes for Hebrew-speaking participants in the program. I also turned out to be the best male dancer of the international leadership training group. I felt honored when the Israeli folk dance instructor asked me to choose the best female dancer as a partner for the dance portion of the graduation ceremony, about the return of the exiles to the biblical Promised Land, the newly independent Israel.

What a wonderful sense of privilege, and to be in love!

LOSS

One cold winter night of 1953, my red-haired queen was meeting an esteemed fellow member from her right-of-center Zionist movement. This already made me anxious. My anxiety mushroomed, not knowing whether he was a potential threat or a former lover. I decided to hide under a row of short bushes facing the door to her building, with a pounding heart for their return, shivering with unhinged jealousy. I was stiffening in the cold of an unusually snowy Jerusalem winter, overwhelmed by a never, ever before felt state of mind! The *fizz of love,* flattening by my smothering emotion.

Alone, unsettled, I feared the anger cursing through me like an overflowing river from a broken dam. Aloneness, jealousy, a blaming voice cracking the shell of my deluded, unexamined "natural" love.

I never thought about how I loved. The question unbalanced a seemingly easily accessible part of myself! The mind slipped away from my body like flower petals falling off the stem. My sense of aloneness deepened.

My idealizing grounding core was splintering. An unknown *inner* voice spoke, like God speaking to the biblical prophets hiding from his presence: *"Never fall in love with the same passion ever again."*

It was a mean-spirited voice, fragmenting my pursuit for justice, equity, the collective sensibility of belonging. How did these social/ political passions connect to love? I could sense myself drifting from my guiding noble pursuits.

My 19-year-old self-preserving mind waved it away. *"That's life, right? Right!"* I felt the grounding embrace of love loosening, climbing the mountaintop of unforgiving rage that had been icebound from awareness. I pursued my love with what remained of my sexualized erotic wishes, but the anticipation for an everlasting relationship with her was drifting away.

A loveless future had begun!

Our parting goodbye in July at the airport was sad and dry. I never recovered from this very first conscious goodbye to a part of my heart, calcifying.

Thus began a lifetime struggle, drifting into my early 50s. A day-in, day-out life with an entrapped soul, kept out of awareness until just before my 90th birthday.

It saddens me to put words to this conscious awareness of loss. *I lived in doubt, in sadness denied, in the solitary enclosure of fear, rationalized.*

SEDUCED

During the summer of 1954, a precociously alluring 17-year-old girl seduced me when I ventured a visit to my old Habonim summer camp during the college summer break. I have a vague sense of being looked up to by this energized young girl. I was all of 20, which was considered an older generation within the youth movement.

Desire, a splinter of the connected body/mind pierced the hardness of my mean-spirited coverup. She went back home, and I joined her for the remainder of the summer school break. The pleasure of orgasms guided my 20th year.

Her family's apartment living room had a view of the Great Lake, with a plush cushioned couch and matching cushioned armchairs facing the fireplace. The adjoining dining room doors through which we entered had etched glass panes. The dining room windows also looked out on the Great Lake. My poverty-focused eyes kept widening to privilege, to etched glass-paneled doors. I was seduced by the comforts of wealth.

Opposite the windows was a swinging door, through which the cook emerged to serve us chicken fricassee, announced with a festive glee by the girl's father as the cook's southern specialty. *Why was the father honoring the servant? I questioned the festive glee voice regarding the working-class serving their masters! I judged it as manipulative, regardless of the ease with which it was announced. The view of the Great Lake narrowed.*

After dinner, the girl's father took the hand of the stunningly beautiful woman sitting to his left to walk down a long hallway. My eyes glued on the dark-haired, tall, slender, exquisitely curved woman as they entered the master bedroom closing the door behind them. We went into my spirited girlfriend's bedroom, closing the door behind us.

Envy, I can now state, is a lot cooler than jealousy!

The following morning, I was introduced to the other side of the dining room swinging door: a large kitchen with an adjoining long pantry room with its own small window. Shelves loaded with cans, bottled grains, and cartons of food. A storehouse of plenty adding to the comforts of wealth. The shadow on the lack in which I grew up became darker. I was losing myself in their entitlements.

How would I ever measure up to the affluence of entitlement? My self-view widened my ignorance by imagination.

The next morning, she told me that her mother was hospitalized with an emotional breakdown. I listened in disbelief; *her mother in the hospital with a nervous breakdown! Why wasn't she more distressed?*

She was relating facts to me like notes for a novel, adding to my moral imbalance. *Why is this eldest of three daughters, so at ease to accept her father's affair for me to witness, while the mother is hospitalized?* Father and daughter functioned with a set of standards distinctly different from how I was raised!

My ethical sensibilities once again got pushed aside in order to continue to enjoy sexual pleasure. I'm recalling Stanley Kubrick's film, *Eyes Wide Shut,*[1] dealing with the necessity for masks and secrets in relationship. My seductress was looking forward to the fall freshman

---

1 *Eyes Wide Shut* is a 1999 erotic mystery/psychological drama film directed, produced and co-written by Stanley Kubrick. It is based on the 1926 novella *Traumnovelle (Dream Story)* by Arthur Schnitzler, transferring the story's setting from early 20th-century Vienna to 1990s New York City.

year at a highly esteemed, prestigious university. The boyfriend of a close friend was practicing for the international Brahms piano competition. These were individuals competing in the world as if it was their oyster!

To support myself while back at school, I found a sales job in a shoe store. It was all right except for the occasional smelly feet disgusting me. Hearing from his daughter of my revulsion moved her father to get me hired as a busboy in the professionally sought-after, not-antisemitic clubs he belonged to in town. I was happy to enjoy the free delicious lunches which were included in the job. I recall whistling softly the overture from *La Forza del Destino,* an opera by Verdi, while picking up plates, forks, knives and glasses, letting the privileged diners know that their busboy was cultured! No one ever commented. It was my own private game, in search of recognition.

I lived in a below street-level apartment. I did charcoal drawings on three of the walls: Moses holding the two 10 Commandment tablets; a woman cradling an infant in her arms; and a third of a beautiful woman to love...a graphically condensed version of my inner struggle.

I couldn't speak! I could only choose nonverbal ways to convey my conflicting emotions. Drawings of laws to live by, cradled tenderness, and a wished-for icon to love. I tried to fly high for two months that summer, despite my confusion and repressed guilt.

Does self-appropriated entitlement deal with anything everlasting, beside the wishing of a desiring self?

I felt challenged to be more than I was. Only now can I entertain the thought that the girl was enjoying me to gratify her own entitled freedom. I was obviously entrapping myself in the oyster-shell world I imagined they lived in. How would I meet the challenge of this seemingly limitless mindset?

I kept wishful thoughts lit like neon lights to contend with the darkness of fear.

I decided to put myself up for the draft to benefit from the wartime Korean GI bill. The armistice with North Korea had been signed. I wasn't taking any chances. It would support a high-level professional education, qualifying me for status and the supposedly freewheeling lifestyle needed to prop up my aspiring self.

Wishing and rationalizing were embracing like conjoined twins. *My collective sensibilities for repairing the world, fading in the throes of my longed-for future.*

Was I living in a garden with fruit hanging from the tree of accomplishments? *Was all of this planning a cover up for acknowledging being used and using? Does obsessive planning obscure the harsh fact of not knowing what to do; admitting to who I am?*

FREE WILL

The Army was a totally unfamiliar world. As we spit-polished our boots in the latrine after lights out, a guy from the back country hills of Kentucky told us, "I'm tired of the Army, it's not what I expected. I'm not coming back after our upcoming three-day pass."

I reacted with, "The CID [Criminal Investigative Department] will come after you and you'll spend two years in the brig."

"They'll never find me," he said.

"What do you mean?"

"I'll know two weeks ahead of time if anyone has come into the area looking for me."

No one else spoke. I thought he was lying to himself. I knew nothing of the hills of Kentucky beyond the zither-playing John Jacob Niles,[2] who gave a concert at my college. Where did he get the confidence with which he shared what he planned to do? Another unfamiliar world for my awakened ignorance to make sense of.

It strikes me how this back-country Kentuckian was *born free!* What do intellect, money in the bank, social status or talent have to do with "Free Will"?

---

2 John Jacob Niles (1892-1980): folklorist, balladeer renown for "I Wonder as I Wander," a Christmas hymn.

It would never have crossed my mind that there are people whose sense of self is beyond the constraining boundaries I grew up with. Is this free will genetic, or an appropriated delusion in each of us?

At this point in my life, aware of genetically-endowed sensory, proprioceptive, brain neurology, individuality, declaring the free will of my Kentuckian soldier-in-arms seems clearly an appropriated delusion, culturally embraced like a prejudice or superstition. But it was a shocker when he declared it with such an unassuming confidence!

It was shortly thereafter that a "Dear John" letter arrived from my teenage seductress during the initial eight weeks of basic training. She hoped I would understand that she had fallen in love with an aspiring astrophysicist. I was set back! But it didn't take long for the forgotten, mean-spirited voice to speak.

"You didn't fall in love with the same passion, did you?" I said to myself. *Love motion* bubbles flattening even more by what next might happen.

That's the way it goes. Loss "comes and goes, speaking of Michelangelo"—borrowing words and rhythm of a line from the poem "The Love Song of J. Alfred Prufrock" by T. S. Eliot.[3] As the French say, *c'est la vie,* or as my fifth-grade friend uses for her computer password, *ah zoi iz es*: Yiddish for "that's the way it is."

Desire was now added to a calculating caution about love. The connection between mind and body, between thought and feeling, separating like the walls of a canyon. The Army kept whisking me away from my unexamined self.

Unlike the witch in the Snow White fable, I wasn't asking the mirror to speak to me. "Just get-on with it! Survive." I sensed the unspoken

---

3 The esteemed American-born poet T.S. Eliot was living in England when he wrote "The Love Song of J. Alfred Prufrock: in 1917.

words of my father; I had yet to experience them emotionally, many years later.

Years later, married and re-married, with married children and growing grandchildren, while turning the pages of the *New York Times* I landed on her obituary. I was surprised to see a lengthy detailing of my highflying girlfriend's professional achievements as a professor of the microscopic workings of our body cells. It mentioned her divorce from the publicly celebrated astrophysicist who explained the galactic ingredients that are a part of our body's evolutionary makeup. *How ironic,* the thought crossed my mind, *that these celebrated, accomplished researchers and professors delving into the motion of cells in body, in space-time couldn't form a lasting bond of intimacy.*

ARTIST

The self-doubt I experience from my two failed romances receded out of mind as the new challenging encounters of Army life were consuming my formerly innocent energy.

Deeply affective emotional events were replaced by memories, for creative interpretations. Balloons to be juggled in public!

I can now refer to what was happening as denied anger and sadness. *Life goes on, right? The empty hollow in my soul had fallen in the forest of forgotten dreams.*

A disassembling of that which I never doubted ensued during the Fall of 1955-56. My accumulated skills and knowledge bounced around like pinballs, keeping me sufficiently in the game of reality.

While standing in line in Seattle, awaiting assignment to the Far East, I heard the soldier behind the counter repeatedly shouting out "K" for Korea to one soldier after another. I quickly decided when I stood in front of him to blurt out about my high school technical training. He paused to look at my personnel file before saying "J" for Japan.

I found myself on Etajima, a small island 20 minutes off the coast of what was the major shipbuilding city of Kure, Japan. Kure was the intended site for the atomic bomb instead of Hiroshima. I can't recall how this came to my attention, but it made sense as it was the major shipbuilding site for Japan's naval superiority in the Pacific Ocean.

Etajima was the American training center for staff stenographers and for construction surveyors, for which I was being trained. Finally, a productive job of plotting roads and building sites while in the Army. We were settled in the former Japanese Naval Academy vacated by the British when their southwest command moved out onto Kure. The campus was expansive, with grand old Greek revival buildings and a church into which I would occasionally just sit in a subdued, unspeakable loneliness.

The training was easy because of my algebraic engineering courses. I enjoyed discovering the adjoining small town outside the Academy for beer guzzling and carousing.

I borrowed books for the Japanese man who ran the laundry. The young Japanese woman who worked with him, who spoke a halting English, eventually invited me for an afternoon lunch at her apartment in town. I anticipated a seductive tryst, another fruit to be picked and remembered. It turned out to be a lengthy, talky lunch with her playing the *koto*, a 13-string instrument on a board that lies on the floor. Considering my anticipated expectation, her playing was only plucking sounds, lost on me. I couldn't hear what she was playing for me. I was caught up in the "life goes on" rationale to deal with my unfulfilled fantasies and loss.

Our senses dampen when love disappears, as we hover in mid-air with anticipated wishes!

I took a subsequent trip to devastated Hiroshima, with unsmiling faces. I went to listen to the New York Philharmonic, led by Leonard Bernstein, as part of the dedication of the newly completed cultural center. I also sat through a traditional tea ceremony, and I couldn't fathom why it took so long!

I was fortunate to get a three-day pass after a hospital stay with pneumonia, from which I awakened one day, startled, to look at the concrete narrow paths outside, totally pink with fallen cherry blossoms. I can still recall my stunned reaction to this scene of utter beauty, 60 years later. I had never seen anything like it.

Finally, I was able to use the three-day pass to see Kyoto, with its exquisite temples. I had long wished to visit the city, having seen Marlon Brandon in the film *Sayonara*, based on the novel of the same name by James Michener; a story about the love between the son of an Army general and a featured star of the fabulous Takarazuka company in Nara, a short ride from Kyoto.

Takarazuka was an all-female company performing a combination of musical numbers, traditional Kabuki scenes, and the emotionally-stirring classical Noh drama theater that preceded Kabuki, ending the show with a Radio City leg-kicks lineup. I loved it. I stood outside after the performance to look at the all-female cast dressed in their daily kimonos walking away from the theater, rekindling my romantic longing for the sentiment of *falling* in love.

The lingering fantasy of being absorbed by romance reappeared like a spider's web to ensnare my inner self like the pink pathway. In retrospect, I was in love with love, with make-believe!

I spent three months in Etajima, experiencing dynamic, cultured, intriguing Japan asking to be engaged with, then ended up in Korea demanding to be lived through. The 24th Division in Korea lost 600 men going home. I was one of the numerical replacements. The biggest building in Seoul at the time was the train station, built sometime after the Japanese occupied the country in 1910. It was a totally patriarchal society while I was stationed there.

The pleasures of the new, shadowed by the past, seesawed during my first year and half of Army life. I did get to set up a library for the headquarter company of my 21st infantry battalion, because I knew the Dewey system for organizing fiction and non-fiction books. The battalion's A company was on the DMZ, the demilitarized zone. I managed to read 50-some books in three months, sipping away on scotch that an Army career Master Sargent bought for me at the officer's club. I wrote lengthy letters to friends back in the U.S. as if we were forever bonded. *It was an imagined and serviceable bonding for my denied fear and underlying anxiety lingering in the arid soil of aloneness. I lived with endless reflections about life in my loveless meandering.*

The freezing winter of '55 turned to the spring of '56, with my discharge on the horizon. Confused, without any plan or direction, I shocked myself on a liquored night declaring, "I'm going to be an artist!"

Artist at what? echoed the Greek chorus of the mind.

"A choreographer. A bodily language understood internationally by all." An instinctual dialogue with myself leapt into a conscious determinism. The parched soil opened to a flowering seed; passionate intimacy transformed into an independent self-proclaimed artist.

The inner voice was merging with my embedding musculature guarding the secrets of love and loss. Framing this beginning as *to be an Artist* attested to my wish for recognition for my inner-self *as distinct from* my idealized, over determined sense of belonging.

I turned consciously to visually projected images. The books I read were paying off, especially the Thomas Mann classic, *The Magic Mountain,* about a man and a woman invalided with tuberculosis in a Swiss sanitarium falling in love in three pages (written in French, which I never got translated), overcoming the inevitable certainty of death by surrendering to the chaos of love.

My second marriage just happens to be to a beautiful, elegant French woman. Is that an accident? A coincidence? Questions I never

22

considered before! Like so much that has happened in my professional life, and most especially in my late 80s, recovering from Covid.

Perhaps artistic displacement began earlier. I had been praised during my adolescence and teen years for my dancing ease. I had in fact choreographed the breakdown between Moses and Korah[4] for a yearly fund-raising program while in Habonim, the Zionist youth movement.

The Choreography:

Moses and Korah enter shoulder-to-shoulder stamping a rhythmic pattern of solidarity in the exodus from Egypt. As they reach center stage, Moses unexpectedly is taken over by his *inner prophetic* calling, breaking the shoulder bond with Korah to descend to the floor and sit with hands to his temples into a private *inner space.*

Korah, abandoned by Moses' sudden break, starts stamping the bonding rhythms of solidarity, hoping to conjure Moses back, then spins aimlessly without purpose or direction. Moses slowly uncoils, arms raised to heaven, totally unresponsive to Korah. Korah drops to the floor as if swallowed by the earth into a fetal position rolling off stage.

Moses resumes the Exodus rhythm quietly with a focused determination facing the audience while extending an open

---

4 In Numbers 16, Korah, a close relative of Moses and Aaron who desires Aaron's position of high priest, leads a rebellion against Moses as the Hebrews journey from Egypt to the Promised Land. As punishment, the earth swallows him up alive.

palm to them, the other arm reaches up to his inner god into the heavens.

The spotlight narrows to blackout.

A short non-verbal version of Korah questioning Moses' God-given authority. A critical challenge between the communal bonds and the internally unquestionable spiritual sacred bond. A fascinating episode in the Exodus from bondage to the land of milk and honey, the Promised Land.

Moses' union is with *I Am*—the name God tells Moses to use when questioned by the Pharaoh, "Who is this god?" Moses' inner dialogue with God is what made his dismissive response to Korah unavoidable. Many years later I discovered that Korah, also from the tribe of Levi, was his blood cousin!

I wonder, was my capacity for condensing, abbreviating the details of reality, already working at 16? I just assumed that everyone would understand the shoulder-to-shoulder synchrony of rhythms as a merger in aims; the symbolism of descending lower and lower as an internal reflexive private meditative dialogue with God; aimless spinning as confusion; emphatic stamping as determination; the arm upward, then to the audience, a pleading invitation to follow his assigned journey.

It seemed so obvious and practical to me. I was, in retrospect, unconsciously making use of my technical schooling about Time > *rhythms*, and Space > *directions*. Korah falling to the ground as consumed by the darkness of abandonment. Moses endowed with a mission to free the Israelites after his burning bush encounter with God.[5] Korah, a Levite, had reached a privileged position as a supervisor,

---

5 Moses and the Burning Bush, Exodus 3:2-5 KJV.

with authority, believes his solidarity with the Exodus assures him a continuing special status. He is however confronted by Moses' obeisant union, dashing his belief in the implicit loyalty of familial relationship.

Moses' unquestioning belief in the mystical unity with God protected his abandoned rage, when he kept beating the rock that God told him to tap with his staff for water to gush forth for the thirsty. Or when, in a rage, the Commandments fell from his hands upon his seeing a golden calf built in his 40-day absence as a shameless surrender to the Egyptian idol worship, contradicting the creation of an Abrahamic monotheism that the non-Hebraic slaves had inculcated following their liberator, Moses. The earth opened to swallow the disloyal to the faith.

The commandment "I am your God, your only God" is a private self-experience. It has no image.

Moses was to discover that because of those moments of uncontrollable rage, God would forbid him entry to the land of milk and honey.[6]

It's clear, as I've aged, that neither rage nor obedience can recover the sweet colostrum that feeds the infant's innocent attachment to the loving maternal object that is the driving power of belief in the omnipotent.

In hindsight, my choreography was a foretelling of my own powerful infantile love, that I experienced as *never questioning how I loved*. It was an innocent, unwitting disclosure of my evolving character—*the unquestioned motion of intimacy, the liberating dance of independence, the pleading gestures of loneliness*!

It took me a long time to coalesce the personal, nonverbal sacred with the communal familial language. There were many unspoken, hidden conflicts and behaviors that needed to be revealed, worked

---

6 Deuteronomy, 32:52 KJV.

through, integrated. It takes time that cannot be scheduled nor improvised. *Awareness is a nakedness of spirit, not a nudity of body or mind.*

DOUBT

Uncertainty drove the decision for a college degree. I was afraid to go directly to Hollywood and try my luck as a dancer. I had no formal dance training, in case my single-minded artistic ambition didn't work out. My fear also influenced my unsettling mean-spirited decree to *never love with the same passion* which included the passion to just do, but love I wanted without reservation.

Rational practicality helped me to think about my choreographic aspiration as a performance art, dictating the choice of a theater major focus in the Speech Department. The dance workshop was under the auspices of the Physical Education Department as an uncredited voluntary activity. It was where my aspiring dream belonged.

Theater history opened my mind to its beginnings as biblical storytelling performances on the steps of churches, followed by platform stages in public squares. Early theater eventually evolved into more sophisticated classic characters and plots known as *commedia dell'arte*[7] ensembles. Focus on plots and character resulted in more detailed playwriting and theater stages that the audiences could visually relate to, with wing and fly space for scenery. Set design flourished and lighting followed as technological advances evolved.

---

7 *Commedia dell'arte:* Early form of professional theater popular throughout Europe, 16th-18th century.

I was cast in minor roles in several major theater productions at the university. I learned how to paint backdrops, build sets, and implement the subtlety of lighting to add to the emotional transitions of a play. I discovered the historical changes in acting techniques that led to the more familiar private explorations of Stanislavski,[8] better known in the U.S. as The Method, and the theatrical techniques of his followers: Michael Chekov's[9] Plasticity, and Meyerhold's[10] Constructionism. These ideas and techniques are still used in plays and films today.

My graduation project was to turn a short story about a beggar—by the soulful Yiddish writer I. L. Peretz, which I translated into English— into a scripted monologue, which I wrote, performed, directed and costumed, with complicated make-up and lighting. It was well received, with high marks. I was discovering the historical and practical ways of affecting the private *inner motion of feelings* in the constructed, condensed theatrical time and space.

The stairway to my future profession in how to work as an analyst with anyone's fantasy was already being built through the performing arts. I had a fundamental understanding of how the stairway was constructed, and could choreograph the process without hesitation. However, the way to deeply grasp the emotional needs of the actor's work was yet to come. It is a process that was beyond my bound time/ space grasp at the time. It involves empathy for the actor, not just the character's intentions and physical expressions of the play.

---

8 Stanislavski, Konstantin: a developer of acting theory focused on the physical experience of the character in a play.

9 Chekov, Michael: a follower of Stanislavski who developed a bodily and psychological practice.

10 Meyerhold, Vsevolod: a follower of Stanislavsky who extended the visual impact of gestures, known as biomechanics.

My choreographic dreams found a place in the non-accredited Dance Workshop. I laid in bed one night envisioning in the dark hollow space below the ceiling a solo figure in white being met by a beautiful woman in blue for the first *pas de deux*, then a second duet which also ended in abandonment, in aloneness. *A choreographic version of my failed romances.* I named it *Evanescence of the Heart.* An unwitting fraying of the heart.

I initially choreographed my vision to Stravinsky's anxiety-driven rhythmically-charged *Duo Concertante*. It was an intuitive choice, resonating my anxiety. It didn't dovetail the choreography with the score. Stravinsky's music fed my anxiety. However, the head of the department sensed the discord of love duets and music as two separate emotional realities, and suggested an original score for the Spring concert by a local composer that might be less challenging for the viewer. She also suggested just calling it *Evanescence*. Removing *the Heart*, the organ where I sensed my emotional pain.

As this was my first venture to be judged for a concert, her acceptance was a relief. I didn't speak up, as I might have now.

I wonder as I write, if I had any sense of how I transmuted my pain into memory balls to be juggled as wishes had become?

The following year's Spring Concert resulted in a second choreographic piece, *Afternoon of a Faun*,[11] the only orchestral piece in Carl Orff's *Carmina Burana*, dovetailing the score more closely to celebrate my consciously focused erotic sensibilities. Psychoanalysis calls it sublimation, a form of displacing *inner* into *outer*. All artistic modalities are considered sublimations; artifice representing in movement, as in all art, the private sensory felt feelings of the artist, often unconscious.

---

11 Carl Orff's *Carmina Burana Cantata* (1935-36).

I treated eroticism as the hidden longing of every human soul. It is what I tried to sense while talking to someone, a sense of what the other wishes that I could satisfy. My inner, more isolated, unconscious self always remained apprehensive. The hidden self was constant, split off from what is actually going on inside. A private lonely harbor for an unmoored soul.

I was finding a way to put my romantic tragedies and idealized values out there through dance: imagined partners, passionate gestures, shapes unfurling through empty space. My unresolved turmoil was finding an aesthetic confessional hollow stage for control of longed-for intimacy.

Is applause an absolution for my obsessional terror of loss? Do clapping hands squelch the sound of tears that weren't forming? Lost in loss wasn't bringing me any closer to love.

I was becoming aware of a distinction between an outer celebration and my inner emptiness. It eventually led to the unraveling during my psychoanalysis with thousands of ribbons spewed on the floor.

Discovering the self is like breathing, one just keeps doing it!

IMMERSION IN DANCE

The American Dance Festival

During the summers of 1957 and 1958, I participated in two six-week lighting internships at the American Dance Festival,[12] formerly at Connecticut College in New London, CT. These sessions included two daily modern dance technique classes with the leading modern dance choreographers José Limón, Martha Graham, Merce Cunningham, Alwin Nikolais, and Helen Tamiris teaching her husband's Daniel Nagrin's choreographic technique; classes in composition with Doris Humphrey[13] and Lucas Hoving;[14] music classes with Norman Lloyd;[15] and aesthetics with Ludwig Binswanger[16]...all of which prepared me for acceptance in the dance diploma program at Juilliard in New York in the Fall of 1958, after graduating college with a Bachelor of Arts.

---

12 The American Dance Festival, a prestigious and world-renowned school, celebrated the burgeoning art form of Avant Garde Modern Dance.

13 Doris Humphrey was a seminal choreographer and theoretician, and one of the founders of Modern Dance.

14 The Dutch dancer, teacher and choreographer Lucas Hoving was best known for the original roles he created as one of the original members of the José Limón Dance Company.

15 Norman Lloyd (not the actor) was a composer, teacher, and supporter of the arts who played a significant role in 20th-century American music, in particular for his work scoring Modern Dance and film.

16 The Swiss psychoanalyst Ludwig Binswanger championed the aesthetics of Modern Dance.

I found many new playmates in the whirlwind theater world of auditions and performance. I was living my fantasy life, becoming a part of a new, idealized aesthetic sensibility where I learned new value structures, a new language, new personalities to aspire to. This re-awakened an excitement I thought I had lost. My competitive drive was rekindled, but with a cold eye and a sharpened criticality that seemed so endemic to my new art world.

JUILLIARD

The Juilliard School of Music, formerly on West 122 Street and Claremont Avenue, was the setting for my daily immersion in dance and thoughts about dance. My days included an hour and half of Limón technique with Betty Jones, June Dunbar, Ruth Currier and Michael Hollander,[17] a ballet class with Alfredo Corvino,[18] and adagio class with Antony Tudor.[19] Once a week I studied choreography with Louis Horst,[20] Labanotation with Ann Hutchinson,[21] and Ideokinesis with Lulu Sweigard.[22] In addition, I attended rehearsals in Fred Berk's modern Israeli folkdance company twice a week, including some 20 weekend performances per year. This means I was dancing close to ten hours a day, before the idols of Modern Dance! Perhaps this

17 Principal dancers of the José Limón Dance Company.

18 Corvino was the ballet director of the Metropolitan Opera.

19 Antony Tudor, celebrated British-born dancer and choreographer who founded the London Ballet and developed the form known as psychological ballet, conveying states of emotional conflict, character and motivation.

20 Louis Horst, composer and pianist whose work included matching Modern Dance choreography with pre-existing musical structures, including contemporary music.

21 Ann Hutchinson a.k.a. Ann Hutchinson Guest, was an authority on dance notation and movement analysis. She established the "Language of Dance" approach to dance education.

22 Lulu Sweigard, a leading authority on body alignment and posture, explored the nervous system for efficient neuromuscular interactions in dance and movement.

sounds hyperbolic, but I was still idealizing, just as much as when I aspired to be a part of the pioneering Zionist kibbutz movement.

It may seem obvious to the reader that believing in something or someone as superior, idealization, must begin much earlier in one's life, as I was to eventually to acknowledge…and ultimately, painfully work through.

I got married in 1959 to an attractive, exciting, dark-haired, progressive-minded woman—with a Yiddish background, to "qualify" her in my estimation as safe and close to home. We found a one-bedroom apartment on West End Avenue with a doorman for $100 a month, raised to $106 when a new gas range and refrigerator were added a couple of years later. Not inexpensive at the time. We needed to earn more money.

EARNING A LIVING

I supplemented my GI bill monthly payments with a three-hour Saturday morning Modern Dance teaching job at the Kew Gardens Parent-Teacher Co-op, a program initiated by parents in conjunction with the Queens College Education Department. John Lidstone, who was earning his Ph.D. at the time and later became Dean of the Art Education department, was the acting director for the Co-op program. He was the co-author, photographer and book designer of *Creative Movement for Children: A Dance Program for the Classroom,*[23] the work which established me as an international voice in creative movement.

The Kew Gardens Co-op job shifted my thinking from choreographer-dancer to dancer-teacher. John Lidstone asked me to accept into a class a little six-year-old girl who was unable to give up her crutches, despite repeated assurances from both her surgeon and physical therapist that she was totally healed from a fall—off a horse, if I remember correctly. The sensation of standing on her own two feet that she associated with the pain of falling made it impossible for her to give up the crutches. The frightening memory of falling, the memory of pain, was still too alive in her. The body went missing for this sweet six-year-old!

I reluctantly complied with John's request, knowing that all of the exercises would be done on the floor.

---

23 *New York: Van Nostrand Reinhold, 1969.*

But in doing so, I had begun the circuitous journey back to love!

Fun movement was at the heart of my teaching in a program initially seen merely as a middle-class exposure to culture. Within the 21 Saturdays of the program, the fun-loving atmosphere and approach resulted in the little girl abandoning the crutches, then her cane, finally running around the room with the other girls. The girl's parents were ecstatic about her emotional recovery from the fear which we now call PTSD (Post-Traumatic Stress Disorder).

I was praised at a parent/staff luncheon and asked to speak about how this psychophysical transformation happened. What I'd done was simply a common-sense way to include her. My description of it was matter-of-fact and practical:

After the exercises, I usually explored the freedom of movement. As the other girls were running around the room, I picked her up in my arms and ran around with her. Slowly over the weeks, I lowered her body so that her toes touched the floor while I was still holding her and running, which led to her eventually sensing the balls of her feet, then the whole sole, until she felt the floor totally supporting her weight. Then I stopped running, allowing for everyone to celebrate her accomplishment as she stood on her own two feet!

There was an alarming, deafening silence in the room after my description. I was saved when John quickly emphasized my *natural* teaching gift. One would think that I might have felt uplifted. Instead, I left the luncheon somewhat ashamed by my lack of a more psychological or pedagogic language to describe such a transformative physical and emotional turn around by this child, while reports by other teachers sounded more professional to me. I was envious of their presentations. I had no distance; every person was the imagined extension of my parents, whose pride in me and approval I sought. Psychoanalysis calls it transference.

In retrospect, jealousy, although subdued, continued to meander through my unexamined psyche. My underlying childlike innocence and fear, which preceded the loss of love, kept rearing its head!

I was determined to think more consciously about a pedagogic framework for the following Fall, as if that would be the solution for the jealousy and competitiveness I'd felt as a toddler with my almost-four-years older sister and my father for my mother's total love. It was an unconscious obsession with love and an unrelenting fear of loss. I couldn't quite make the transition from the three-year-old to four, which will be become clearer as my journey unravels.

Playfulness was my connection to my father before the age of ten, when we were still in Cuba, in Habana Vieja, the old part of Havana, before coming to Detroit to join my paternal grandfather.

Recalling his playfulness with an appreciative heart was another unplanned step in my recovery of love.

I wonder whether the simplicity of my caring for the girl by picking her up from the floor, so as not to feel alone watching the other girls, to lowering her feet over time, was too intuitive a way to teach? Or was the silence at the luncheon a deeply felt reaction by everyone beyond applause or words? Perhaps I am finally wise enough to reconsider the emotional resonance of their silence, and not just my sense of inadequacy.

It would be some time before I sensed, and not just used, the non-verbal. I was still a thinker, relying on words and movement. I was my mother's son. She loved words. Her father was a teacher of young children. Tradition! These are intergenerational transmissions silently absorbed into our psychic life, our character.

The affirming praise for my Saturday teaching job led me to seek pick-up concerts with other choreographers, including the celebrated

Charles Weidman[24] for a Philadelphia concert where I met Ray Bolger, the Straw Man in *The Wizard of Oz* film, who told us in the green room that he too improvised creatively all the time in his basement, without a particular aim.

I also made the audition cut from 250 to the last 25 dancers for the film *West Side Story,* with Jerry Robbins sitting in the orchestra deciding who stayed and who went.[25] (Since Hollywood demanded the casting of only SAG—Screen Actors Guild—dancers, I didn't qualify. Jamie Rogers, a Puerto Rican whose sister was already in the road company of the *West Side Story* musical and who had a striking technique, got into the movie.) In addition, the choreographer Fred Berk asked me, while he traveled to Israel that summer, to captain his modern dance company for a television appearance in Toronto and a summer variety dance program in Central Park. These opportunities kept bolstering my self-approval. The Central Park program included the very young Alvin Ailey presenting a theatrical, emotionally moving blues piece with the singer Brother John Sellers. Years later, I spent a few dinners with Brother Sellers at the table of our common theater friends, Jules and Doris Schwerin.[26] A subsequent dinner with my friends once included the world-renowned pantomimist Marcel Marceau, who was going to act the role of the biblical Noah in Jules' film. Marceau talked all evening about politics. We were all leftists. I was living a professional artist's life. Hallelujah, recollections!

---

24 Weidman was co-creator, wth Doris Humphrey, of the theory of Fall and Recovery.

25 Jerome Robbins, renowned choreographer of many Broadway musicals

26 Doris was the composer for *Solomon and Ashmedai,* which I directed and choreographed for the 92nd St. Y. Jules, her husband, was production director of the film *Salt of the Earth* (1954), about Mexican zinc mine workers who called for a general strike and succeeded through solidarity. He was eventually blacklisted in Hollywood.

With the passing years, "never loving with the same passion" continued to cast a shadow. I never admitted how cautious I still was about feelings of intimacy. I had relegated passionate love to erotism. I continued to hide from my wife about "not loving with the same passion." She was the mother of our children, my business partner, co-owner of our West Side brownstone that I worked on tirelessly after work and on weekends using all of my technical experience from high school. Hiding, by inextricably weaving love with desire, and constant work, keeping love out of sight and mind. I hid my continuing longing for my mother's love when she rocked me in her arms singing Rozhinkes Mit Mandlen, *raisins with almonds in Yiddish.*

Life marches on, waving the banner of fame to distract from the bitterness of the grief of failed romances.

IMMERSION DEEPENS: FORM

With the promise to be more pedagogically focused for the Saturday morning classes, I concluded that *Form* distinguishes professional dancers from amateurs. The dancer with the clearest sense of their whole-body while executing gestures of arms, torso or legs was praised by the instructor as well as esteemed by classmates. This held true regardless of whatever dance techniques I studied. *Form* was admired. *Form* was professional! *Form* became my pedagogic aim.

Since I was in classes with people who had been studying dance since they were three or eight or 12, the clarity of my *Form* at 24 was what it was...but not distinct. From my self-preserving perspective, I felt and separated *Form* and *Passion*! They were not the same. This distinction didn't fully crystallize until many years later into a formal awareness and my own eventual techniques as a teacher of creative movement.

The following Fall of 1959, John Lidstone asked me to start a boy's class for ages 6-8. With my pedagogic intent in mind, I turned to what I had learned about Rudolf Laban[27] at Juilliard from Ann Hutchinson. Laban's analytic formulations of what a body in space must work with

---

27 Rudolf Laban was an Austro-Hungarian artist, chorographer, and movement theorist

impressed my orderly physics, chemistry, and engineering high school mindset. Laban contended that the human body is always impacted by two irrefutable factors: *gravity*, a downward force, and *space,* a resistance through which movement must happen. Labanotation was the most graphically inclusive language of movement and music, becoming the sought-after system for most ballet companies around the world to record their repertoire.

All of us naturally accommodate gravity and spatial resistance without thinking about them as we grow and move. Framing them theoretically is understandable, not sensory. Laban theorized on forces that impact our volitional kinetic movement. Laban's theory and exploratory techniques became the driving guidelines for early dance therapy when I explored these modalities.

Years later I discovered that Laban was the son of a Hungarian general. I imagined his looking at the father's maps spread out on a large desk showing where the enemy stood in the way, that made sense to call it, *spatial resistance!* After all, space is open with no particular resistance. He treated space as demanding one push through it or against it. This is purely a speculation; enhancing his abstract metaphoric technical language for me, or sublimating his emotional issues with his father. I wondered!

I recall the Swedish dancer Lucas Hoving, the original Iago character to José Limón's role as the Moor, in Limón's impressive, dramatic classic *The Moor's Pavane.* Lucas taught choreography by asking us to imagine carving space with our gestures, contrasted by forming empty space with our shapes. Marcel Marceau, the celebrated pantomimist, characteristically mimed the *effort* of parting the heavy velour stage curtain, while the equally incomparable pantomimist Jean-Louis Barrault showed the parting of a curtain with an elegant back of the hand gesture passing from one space to another, reminding me of the early Japanese Noh theater that preceded Kabuki. Marceau showed parting as his inner emotional struggle. Barrault showed parting as simply passing from where one is into another space. Gesture is symbolic, as in Balinese and Indian traditional dance.

Another example that comes to mind is the great French painter Henri Matisse's line drawings in later life. He drew a penciled, curving line on paper so definitively that you could see the shape of the object, although the full form was not defined. The delicacy of his penciled line suggested the volume and delicacy of the object. It elicited the viewer's imagination of both the *form* and *feeling* about the Form.

Reminds me of when I was child looking at clouds and imagining faces, animals, landscapes. I couldn't get over the sheer simplicity of Matisse's graphic sensibility! It has stayed with me throughout the years. I recall reading or hearing of Picasso saying after Matisse's death, "Who will I learn from now that he died?"

All pantomime is a literal physical imitation of reality. The curtain is imagined, the door is imagined, the audience imagines along as if they are equally doing, feeling, or distancing themselves by judging how well it is being imagined or consciously devaluing the effort of the imagination. It was only after my frightening Covid experience at 86 when I became sensorially alive to what I felt, without enriching what I see or critically assessing.

I related emotionally to Marceau, and imaginatively aspired to the effortless abstracting Barrault, and literally shed tears falling down my cheeks with Matisse's commentary in his art book, Jazz.

Efforts are a variation of muscle tone, like soft, hard, light, heavy and everything in-between. Muscle tone variations convey the emotional experience of the mover, like a tremor in the voice as we speak telling us of a felt or choked off feeling.

Marceau was telling us that not only was the curtain heavy, but performing, living, is stressful on his soul. Barrault entered space with a toddler's sense of discovery. He was an entitled lover, as I more recently was told by someone who had a first-hand encounter with him. Matisse clearly wrote his book *Jazz* as consciously experiencing when the hand he had trained was out of sync with his soul.[28]

Our brain mirrors muscular effort. The infant senses all of the aforementioned qualities throughout their *whole* body, registering indelibly joy, terror, and everything in-between. This infantile sensibility is never totally lost as we age regardless of the words, we use to qualify the distinctions. It impacts our feelings vibrating thoughts about meaning and intent.

When the *inner motion* of the dancer accompanies the choreography, or the text in acting, we are emotionally moved. We call it, talent!

I was discovering how to teach the mystery of talent. I was discovering the byways of intimacy. Healing myself. from the depression of love lost.

What Laban put together that I found particularly interesting is defining a theoretical framework for the feeling of exhaustion – if we give into *gravity*, we feel heavy. Standing involves a lifting effort that we can theoretically call a *resistance* against gravity. It clearly involves a level of holding muscles, we call strength. These are physical experiential distinctions that imply emotional states of being. They can however be dealt with so concretely that the feeling is suggested but not experienced. Mind, technique, and sensory experience are disjointed.

What seemed rational, simple, insightful to me with my background in physics turned out not to be not so obvious to the seven-year-

---

28 Matisse described it beautifully in his 1947 book *Jazz*, a limited-edition portfolio of printed collages and his written thoughts about them.

old boys in my weekend dance class. I was spending too much time explaining gravity and resistance. Since form and variation of muscle tone, qualities of movement, were my pedagogic curricular focus, I asked them to think of something heavy to show how it moves for the following Saturday. The result of that simple assignment is celebrated in the Wiener/Lidstone collaboration, *Creative Movement for Children: A Dance Program for the Classroom*. The book outlined my dance techniques developed over ten years. I chose the photographic sequences throughout the book showing the improvisational value of the images, along with detailing the focus of all of the exploratory syllabus. John wisely and gratefully edited my run-on associations into intelligible sentences and exquisitely designed pages. The last pages had a graph of ten years of work since my initial discoveries in 1959.

Our book contract with Van Nostrand Reinhold came about because John had written an article for an educational art magazine that included a filmed sequence of one of the boys from the class. Jean Koffed, the editor at Van Nostrand art books who was married to a dancer, was fascinated by the article, and invited us to lunch to discuss the upfront royalty, percentage, and publication schedule for a book.

I was impressed by the restaurant, the chatty conversation between Jean and John, and the wine sipping, all of which had nothing to do with the business details. I was still the little Jewish Cuban boy frozen in poverty, sensing myself totally excluded from the easy banter and shop talk of Jean and John. The book was generated by my explorations that so impressed John as culturally changing ideas for a larger audience of classroom teachers and enriching children. But that separated part of myself still felt excluded.

John used a 35mm camera with a motor that took eight shots per second, capturing the spontaneously improvised movement sequencing of the child. Our contract was extended by three years because of the care involved, making sure that the book showed the instinctual, personal improvisational process elicited by the foci I had come up with to explore qualities of movement that could easily be used by a classroom teacher as a meaningful creative break from sitting. The book sold a thousand copies while still in blues (now called galleys). *I'm going to be rich,* the poor little boy from Cuba thought.

I awaited with anticipation the creativity the boys would demonstrate of something heavy and how it moved for the next Saturday. One boy chose mud, another chocolate pudding, a third an elephant, a fourth the Empire State Building. The improvisations were short, imitative, uninteresting, and discouraging as an exploratory creative technique. They rolled sloppily in the mud, whipped around as pudding, showed a trunk by clasping fingers in front of their body and lifted heavy legs like an elephant or moved stiff bodied like the Empire State building. Some showed the form and activity amusingly. My anticipation of something more innovative was a discouraging downer.

Then, seven-year-old Jeffrey, with his slightly bulkier upper body, chose *clay* as something heavy for an extended number of minutes. When he finished, both I and the Juilliard piano major accompanist glanced at each other, stunned by the consistency with which Jeffrey maintained the heavy quality of clay while continually changing shapes as if he was being sculpted from the inside, while changing spatial levels never losing the internal malleable heavy consistency of clay. The sheer constancy of the malleable heavy quality of *clay* and Form was breathtaking. I wondered, what kept him so together? I imagined a story being played out.

"Were you thinking of something?" I asked when he ended his improvisation. He went on to describe moving in a jungle then chased by a tiger, getting away, falling into a camouflaged pit as the tiger leapt on him. He managed to pull out his knife to kill the tiger.

"Were you thinking of this story before you did your clay?"

"No, it just came to me as I was dancing." I was awestruck, stunned, it was beyond me! I felt like a research scientist with an outlined aim, discovering an unexpected element exceeding his wildest imagination! A waking dream arising out of the *clay* improvisation was startling! An identification with the *clay* image so profound, evoking an environment for the imagined self, like a dream. I was wordless!

I asked the other boys to improvise as *clay*. The results were by and large comparable, as if they all understood physically, emotionally, unconsciously what they saw while watching Jeff. One boy with a slight neurologic disorder must have thought of the class experience over the course of the week and delightfully got it the following Saturday.

I had stumbled onto an awakening that I needed to understand.

My awakening continues to this very day as a psychoanalyst, and with an adult Zoom movement class with just five senior members, one of whom has been a student as far back as 1979.

Creative Movement was no longer just physical inventions, clever imitations, or a kinetically expressed extension of the child's playwriting imagination. Creative movement is an improvisational body foci process generating body/mind/spirit expression.

PROCESS

I needed to understand how this emotionally stunning event happened for Jeffrey and how it was grasped by all the boys in class, like the underground roots of giant redwoods connecting them all. It my accustomed separation of *sensation* (body) *and perception* (mind altered); a separation that seemed so matter of fact as we learn to control intentional movement, kinetic control. Control and intention paradoxically separate us from the earlier sensory body/mind experience of infancy and toddlerhood that feeds idealization later in life.

In a taped interview included in the *Creative Movement* book, John asked Jeff a question: "What is the most important thing you've learned from Jack's class?" Without missing a beat, Jeff simply came out with, "Feeling, the whole secret is feeling."

I teared up, hearing those simple words from Jefferey. When I first heard it on the tape, I had no idea of why the tears came. The notion of feeling was not something I thought about by asking the boys to imagine being something heavy and how it moved. Jeff's explanation forever changed what creative movement is for me. *It was self-discovery! A genuine expression of unconscious feelings, as in dreams. It was art!*

Feeling has remained a guiding focus for all of my explorations, be they dance, directing theater, practicing therapy, experiencing awareness. I claimed credit for what happened because of how I framed the exploration of moving like something heavy. It has taken me a long time to think of what happened as luck, a light lit in my dimmed soul.

My analysis of the criteria that differentiated *clay* from all the other choices the boys came up with eventuated in finding specific images for the other three distinct muscular variations that Laban had formulated. It is amply explained, and photographically shown in the *Creative Movement for Children: A Dance Program for the Classroom* book.

My analysis of the *clay* image, and the subsequent images that conformed with the analysis, was subsequently reinforced by working with after-school classes at two public schools for the next two years, with comparable ages supporting the psychologically generative mind/body/spirit dimensions of the images I had worked out. It was pedagogically fundamental to starting The School for Creative Movement in 1962 with 38 six-to-eight-year-olds. I wasn't only starting a business for a steadier, more assured source of income; I had something meaningful to offer for children's physical and creative growth.

My earlier socio-political ideals had found a new dedication. Teaching *Creative Movement* eventually led me to personal therapy and many years of schooling to be certified as a psychoanalyst. The linking of these two disciplines began in 1962.

I was instinctually reworking my generalized notion of love through teaching. Albeit not integrated on a distinct personal developmental level until many years later.

The book resulted in my giving an hour-long talk at Columbia University's education department; presenting weekend workshops at Syracuse University's Art Education department, renamed Co- and Aesthetic Art to emphasize the sensory aspect of art teaching;

teaching a full day class at the Toledo Museum in Ohio for docents about the object-focused textural eyes of children looking at art; giving two, then three-week summer college-accredited workshops for adults at Quinnipiac College in Hamden, Connecticut, initiated by June Kennedy, arts commissioner of the Connecticut Commission for the Arts, who was moved by the *Creative Movement for Children* book.

The success of the summer programs gave rise to The Institute for Movement Exploration, formed by academic members of those summer workshops, and adopted by Wellesley College for a few years. I continued to offer an all-day Sunday workshop in the fall with some of the summer participants. The two-week summer teacher training at the School on the West Side of Manhattan drew directors of schools from Sweden, Finland, Israel, and practicing creative movement instructors from Brazil, Mexico, Germany, New Zealand, and the U.S. The School for Creative Movement grew to 360 students—210 children ages 3-15 and 150 adults—and had an international reputation by 1974. All classes were limited to ten students as both a personal observational limit and as a financial consideration. My eyes and mind couldn't keep track of more students in a class. A rational sensory process was unfolding modulating an obsessional intellectual tendency.

My work opened the shutters, allowing light into the darkened space of my Inadequacy. Confidence reawakened, I opened myself up further to a sensory process that worked.

Love was not a magical state; it is a living practice.

ACCOMPANYING EVENTS

Prior to the publication of the *Creative Movement* book in early 1969, I had danced in a couple of events for Felix Fibich, an established choreographer of Eastern European Jewish traditional dance, who introduced me to Dovid Licht, the Argentinian Jewish theater director for the Folksbiene Yiddish-speaking theater weekend presentations on the Lower East Side, located on the second floor above the Yiddish daily paper, the *Forverts* (now called *The Forward*) offices and the Workman's Circle offices, owners of the building. The performances resulted in my acting in two plays in Yiddish for two seasons: *Backlane Center* in 1963, and a leading role in the second play, *The Eleventh Inheritor* by Moshe Dluznowski in 1964; I also studied theater directing with the Obie-winning Gene Frankel, who chose two of my class presentations for his weekend public presentations: *The Third Angle* a one-act play by a Canadian woman playwright (whose name escapes me), and *After the Funeral* by I.L. Peretz, translated by me from Yiddish.

I choreographed "Brother, Can You Spare a Dime?"—a number Chad Mitchell selected for his initial solo appearance at The Bitter End (he of the celebrated folk singing group The Chad Mitchell Trio). I also directed and choreographed two fundraising Broadway shows for the B'nai Brith Sisterhood, Chapter One in Brooklyn: Cole Porter's *Anything Goes,* and George Abbott and Douglass Wallop's *Damn Yankees.*

For a National Federation of Temple Youth two-week retreat for 17-to-22-year-olds in Warwick, NY, focused on Jewish artists and Jewish themed art, I directed the world premier operetta production of I.B. Singer's short story, "Gimpel the Fool." Singer—who by then had achieved a widespread English-speaking readership following the 1953 English translation of the story in the *Partisan Review* by Nobel Award-winning author Saul Bellow—was the honored celebrity at this initial gathering. He was pleased with the production.

The success of the *Gimpel* presentation led to an impressed audience member, Cantor Smolover, recommending me to his friend Maurice Friedman, the American translator of Martin Buber. Friedman was being honored by the philosophy department of Manhattanville College of the Sacred Heart with a production of *Elijah,* Martin Buber's only play; a morality play about a struggle with one's soul. This was Buber's *Elijah,* fearlessly confronting the king with truth and willing to pay the price.

Buber's lifetime work influenced many, many people struggling with these profound human issues, including Martin Luther King, Jr.[29] Buber was a lifetime friend of Gershom Scholem, referenced earlier in *Major Trends of Jewish Mysticism.* I was hired to direct and choreograph the play, with a budget for an original score, set designer, costume designer, and a lead actor. It was reviewed by the esteemed leading Broadway theater critic of the former New York Herald Tribune Walter Kerr. *"Broadway comes to Westchester"* was his memorable quote.

---

29 King referenced Buber's "I and Thou" principle in his 1963 "Letter from a Birmingham Jail" to President Lyndon Johnson; the latter was one of the defining statements of the American Civil Rights movement.

ISAAC BASHEVIS SINGER

Bruce Davidson, the celebrated still photographer, ventured into film by combining a short story by I.B. Singer with documentary material. Singer lived two stories below him at the Belnord, an impressive inner courtyard building that wrapped around Broadway, east to Amsterdam, north from 86th to 87th street, and back to Broadway. Other notable residents of the Belnord were Zero Mostel, Walter Matthau, and Yiddish novelist and playwright Moshe Dluznowsky, in whose play *The Eleventh Inheritor* I was given a principal role at the Folksbiene theater. (The Belnord was used for the exterior shots of the fictional "Arconia" apartments on the TV show *Only Murders in the Building*.)

Bruce, knowing that I had directed the *Gimpel the Fool* operetta, asked me to play both Mr. Pupko and Mrs. Pupko, the only acting roles in "Isaac Singer's Nightmare and Mrs. Pupko's Beard." The film was initially shown at the original New Yorker Theater on Broadway and 89th Street, founded by Dan Talbot to show classic Hollywood and foreign films, with live commentary by Peter Bogdanovich, who was earning his PhD at Columbia at the time. The film was subsequently shown on PBS, and then again on PBS after Singer received the Nobel Prize for Literature in 1978. Singer was proud of the first-ever acceptance speech in Yiddish, televised internationally at the Nobel Awards ceremony.

The composer *for Gimpel the Fool* was Cantor Charles Davidson. A cantor friend of Charles, Solomon Mendelson, approached us after seeing the production of *Gimpel* to create an I.B. Singer musical for Broadway. His enthusiasm surprised me. I wondered whether the staging of two distinct spaces—for the taunting, sadistic townspeople front stage left, and Gimpel's private love and pain surreal space up stage right—significantly heightened his excitement theatrically? The limitations of wing, fly space, and lighting highlighted the counterpoint of movement, chorus, and solo arias to work beautifully.

I need to remind the reader that the performers were junior and senior high schoolers, and college freshman and sophomores. Charles' music and my direction and stage framing of the production worked seamlessly together; we were a great team.

Mendelson was responsible for producing a presentation at Beth Sholom Synagogue in Long Beach, NY of Martin Luther King's renown 1963 "I Have a Dream" speech at the Lincoln Memorial, narrated by Ruby Dee and featuring the music of a well-known classical composer. The synagogue had among its membership a number of RKO executives, professionally astute about theatrical productions that included such classic films *as King Kong* (1933) and *Citizen Kane* (1941). Mendelson's suggestion for a Broadway musical carried some weight.

Singer's story captured the human inner struggle with desire, shattering the grounding boundaries of family and social mores. Singer sensed and enjoyed thinking about psychological perversions. The Yiddish-speaking readership of the Daily Forward treated Isaac's perversive literary output dismissively, in contrast to the work of his culturally and politically sophisticated novelist brother, Israel Joshua Singer. The typesetter of the popular Forward newspaper, a practicing orthodox Jew, took the liberty to edit the more blatantly pornographic words and sentences of Singer's stories. However, the growing, psychologically subjective focus of Western culture dovetailed more closely with the sensibilities of the Nobel committee. Time was on Isaac Singer's side!

I made clear to Mendelson that we needed a cohesive libretto/book/script to pull together the elements of drama, song, and dance for a Broadway musical. Davidson's music, using Singers words, worked well for the libretto. I suggested a left-leaning poet friend Eric Blau, might be a good choice to write the book. Eric and I read and analyzed countless Singer stories over several weeks before choosing one we agreed on. We worked closely to outline the theatrical and emotional continuity of scenes, dance, and songs for a two-act musical. Our choice of story expressed our socio-political sensibilities, including graphic imagery for a set designer.

Eric's wife and mine had met at a Lamaze birthing program that led to stimulating dinners together. Our sons were born days apart. Eric's wife, Elly Stone was a regular part of the West Greenwich Village folk music heyday. She was the featured star of *Jacques Brel is Alive and Well and Living in Paris*.

With the outline in place, I refocused on my other pursuits. I was so busy with founding the first creative movement school on the West Side of New York—working evenings initiating the premier evening Board of Education Creative Performing Arts Center on the West Side at PS 199; acting on weekends with the Yiddish-language Folksbiene theater on the Lower East Side; working on the renovation of our brownstone—that I didn't think of calling Eric about his work on our two-act musical book. It was an exciting creative period. Directing and choreographing a Broadway musical would have established me to pursue a career in theatrical direction.

I naively waited trustingly for Eric's call. It never came! As far as I knew, contracts with Mendelson were yet to happen.

I discovered only when Mendelson told me that he had taken around Blau's finished book to established, successful Broadway producers like David Merrick and Gary Cohen who rejected it. Frustrated by whatever conversations he had with Blau, Mendelson called me to analyze what was wrong with the book. He also told me that Eric had received $2000 for his work from him. I was shocked by Eric's theft of our mutual efforts by claiming sole credit, in addition to backstabbing me by telling Mendelson that the show needed a known name like Jerry Robbins to direct and choreograph.

The deceit was unforgivable, adding to my losses of love.

The loss touched another aspect of self so deeply embedded in me that the emotional working through was at times suffocatingly unbearable, needing to be cracked like an egg, until my 90th year. I was dealing with a bottomless pit of self-denials which I had waived away throughout countless years as balls to be juggled, stories to be told to intimate friends I trusted. Was I making assumptions so as not to face myself?

Recounting this episode returns me to my former trusting innocence, when I believed that my childhood was totally carefree. Aspects of self that I would eventually confront with terrifying pain.

Returning to the Mendelson call, I quickly thought about his unwitting deceit with Blau, and I negotiated an up-front fee for my analysis of the rejections by the well-known Broadway producers. He agreed to pay me. When I read Blau's version, it was immediately clear to me that the nonmusical dialogue scenes were out of sync with the emotional flow of Singer's story. These major Broadway producers sensed the script's mismatch and immediately rejected it as unacceptable.

Blau's reputation as a cheat was subsequently confirmed by my composer novelist friend, Doris Schwerin. Doris was the musical composer for *Solomon and Ashmedai*, based on a poem by the renowned Hebrew poet Chaim Nachman Bialik, for which I was contracted as the premier production for a children's series at the 92nd St. YMHA. She told me of a similar backstabbing by Blau, as experienced by a friend of hers. Eric had a track record.

At one point, Blau asked me to direct his production of *Jacques Brel is Alive and Well and Living in Paris* at the Village Gate. The weekly pay of an Off-Broadway contract was pitifully inadequate, plus it interfered with the start of Fall term classes at the school, which he would not negotiate. I refused, and I'm glad I did, as he probably would have tried to control the directorial work. I never bothered to see the show, or to speak to him when our gaze met while walking past each other on Broadway.

Mendelson was so taken by my detailed analysis that he followed my suggestion to approach Singer directly for another story for a Broadway musical. *As I recount this event, the story brings up the supposition that Blau probably managed to contractually reserve his rights as playwright. It also speaks to me of my naïveté about my "natural" relational instincts.*

Since Singer knew me as the director of *Gimpel the Fool* and from the film of Davidson's *Pupko* documentary, he responded to the invitation to meet at the Broadway dairy restaurant just a couple of blocks south of his apartment. After telling Isaac about his substitution of flies or mosquitoes that need scratching as the physical voices of Satan, I asked Singer to choose a story he liked for a Broadway musical. I suggested that he write the dialogue, that I always found emotionally poignant, for the scenes that would lead to songs and dances. "I don't know anything about musicals," Singer admitted. "I will detail a two-act musical with scenes for you to follow," I assured him. Singer agreed.

I delivered the outline on a Sunday morning into his hands at his apartment. Once again, I waited for his response, but didn't hear from him until we met with Mendelson and the retired RKO executives on the tenth floor of the Ansonia Hotel on Broadway and 73rd Street. I sat quietly listening to Singer read the whole script in total disbelief. He had reversed the acts. *I was livid. Singer committed the same unforgivable sin as Blau.*

His reversal was based on his notion that characters need to be introduced before the central conflict is shared with the audience; an older, traditional format for most plays. He had no sense of the emotional framework out of which song and dance express the feelings of the story line. He knew about obsessive desire, about rationalizing, and his own impulsive compulsions. He had a fertile imagination like a young child, but the loving heart and sensory body were somewhere else for Singer.

Musical formats had changed in 1947 with Rogers and Hammerstein's *Carousel*, highlighting the circumstances in which the characters lived, struggled, and loved. Just as in the more recent *West Side Story*, in which the confrontation between the Puerto Rican "Sharks" and the white American "Jets" establishes the cultural mismatch for the tragic romance of Maria and Tony. Singer's reversal didn't follow the emotional plot's progression, making for an ending that didn't ring true. Once again, his changes resulted in rejections. There was no follow up. Compounding my fury was my ignorance of legality; we were working without a contract. My unresolved childhood conflicts continued unconsciously.

Singer was a conflicted moralist, an observer of how morality goes awry amid the itch of wanting, which plagued his life. He had no intrinsic sense of the need to express, in movement or music, the unspeakable voiceless feelings of love, loss, grief and rage. He had been raised to follow laws, orthodox rules; steeped in 613 deeds that a Jewish male is obligated to fulfill every day. His liberation came from storytelling. He unconsciously repressed the earlier emotional developmental experience that is closer to the toddler's sensorial relatedness to the environment and parents, the universe before a *me from you* materializes. Martin Buber's *I and Thou* touches our hearts in conveying this loving universe to which I was powerfully connected; a universe that intuitively flowered in my work as a creative movement teacher before I became a psychoanalyst.

A number of years later, I confronted Singer while he was having lunch with his wife Alma at our local Greek diner on Broadway and 87th St. He didn't remember my having given him a detailed outline. I stood in front of him, watching his eyes widen when I accused him in Yiddish of stealing: *Eer haut es geganvent frum mir, uhnd ir gedenkt nisht?* He reacted in his accented English with, "As Goht is my vitness, I voudn't do a ting like thad."

I unhesitatingly responded, "God is a witness to your theft." Then I departed to join my adult students for lunch. It was my last encounter with Isaac.

Although Yiddish was my language at home from birth, and teaching Yiddish was my work in Jewish after-school programs while at college—plus I performed as an actor in Yiddish theater—I did not celebrate Singer's prideful Yiddish Nobel Prize speech for literature a few years later. I had encountered his true immoral character, regardless of his celebrated storytelling talent.

Why didn't I confront him earlier, you might ask? I still recall looking at a shocking indented crease on his skull while I sat on the stage with the cast after the *Gimpel* production, listening to him as he stood below to speak to the assembled students, staff, and invited guests. At the time, I thought of the crease metaphorically, as an opening to his creative soul! It made him seem really old in my eyes. True, he was the honored Jewish artist of this summer gathering. But what really made me hold back then was *derech eretz*, literally a *path on the earth*, the way of the land. In this case, the "way" was to show respect to one's elders. There are still many cultures where this sensibility is honored. Raised by European Jewish parents, this ethos was ingrained in me.

I have come to recognize that the child in me was treating the self-appropriated arrogance of artists—including my own—as justifiable. Maybe this is my hyperbolic projection of inadequacy, of rage denied on my part. When I finally got around to experiencing my rage in my analysis, it became clear why it was denied. The pain, the shame the implicit dismissal of love, the loneliness is unbearable. It takes a self-aware adulthood to process the pain of loss, the separation from the garden of Paradise where God is a sensed presence.

I was a child happy to work with my Tate (Father), to befriend, to please. One doesn't sign contracts with those early emotional improvised parents. Reconsidering my rationalization upon reading the editing years later, my father didn't engage my competitiveness with him, to help me think more consciously—in the same way that he didn't engage his feelings of abandonment by his father.

Grasping this early love and loyalty—just days ago as I write these words—liberated my self-blame about the run-ins with Blau and Singer. I slept soundly that night.

THE SCHOOL FOR
CREATIVE MOVEMENT

The intensity of Juilliard during the summers of 1959-60 led to teaching choreography for the Board of Education summer programs on the West Side of Manhattan, followed by being asked to be the initiating teacher-in-charge of the Board of Education West Side Adult Performing and Creative Arts program at P.S. 199, for the new Lincoln Towers complex of apartments and the area's burgeoning population. We offered classes in a variety of art mediums; movement techniques including social dance; creative writing; professional bridge classes; plus we made room for the West Side Opera company and the West Side Symphony. Scheduling teachers and classes, establishing administrative fees, hiring office help, choosing a governing board, and overseeing a public relations committee seemed to evolve smoothly over a couple of years.

Now married with a child on the way, my wife and I moved into the garden floor of a brownstone, which we eventually bought when a second child arrived to grace our lives.

Albeit that I was developing a reputation as a theater director in New York, our sustaining financial source of livelihood was the School for Creative Movement. Founding and directing SCM was another unwitting shift away from the self-absorbing singularity of "artist" towards a more implicitly related way of functioning.

The path to rediscovering love continued to reveal itself to me, unwittingly, through teaching.

In the second year of SCM, I began to enroll five-year-olds. When I tried using the winning *clay* image identificatory technique, it simply didn't work with them. A sustained sense of *form* combined with *qualities* of muscular variations, was not yet a way of sensing movement for the fives; too cerebral was a combination of muscular variations, which these younger children naturally internalize and make their own, as they do with parental anxiety or relaxed parental character styles.

I was learning about the developmental changes in bodily self-experience; about the emotional and cognitive changes that occur during those early years. I was becoming less single-minded about *what* had to learned and more focused on *how* it could be learned. The pursuit of the improvisational aspect of creative movement required a shift in my thinking. How five-year-olds feel themselves together has more to do with what they wish or imagine, in contrast with what they are sensing

These understandings were engendering a more compassionate sensibility for me, a path back to love in ways I wasn't aware of and would eventually come to recognize.

MY CONCEPTUAL MODEL

I had formulated a conceptual model for all dance education when I founded SCM, namely *Line, Form, Qualities, Space, and Time.* Regarding the fives, I thought of what precedes *form*, the focus for the six-to eight-year-olds. It was *line*, since *form* wasn't working.

In ballet classes, *line* was often spoken of as a connection from one point to another, the way the hand is sensed connecting to the elbow and then to the shoulder, and so on. An Academy Award-winning animated short film, "The Dot and the Line,"[30] shows how a period, *a dot* becomes a *line,* and how connecting *lines* become a *shape.* From my physical observing perspective, the *line* was commonly imaged visually. A *shape* is more conceptual, a more mentalized visualization of the whole body.

My unacknowledged self-absorbing tension—or anxiety as I now call it—imagined *line* as a *cable,* giving you some idea of what taking ballet classes at Juilliard felt like for me. At 24, I was already too old for the discipline. I was living with too much free-floating passion, and my colorful way of speaking about constant anticipation.

My "cable" reference is indicative of my own skeletal/visual thinking tendency; and the implicit muscular tension of anxiety with which I functioned. I used to think of anxiety as the energy of excitement.

---

30 "The Dot and the Line: A Romance in Lower Mathematics" (1965) was produced by Chuck Jones (of Bugs Bunny fame) and Les Goldman, narrated by Robert Morley. Based on the 1963 book written and illustrated by Norman Juster.

Amazing how easily we can reverse an emotional reality to please or fool ourselves.

When we say that someone is coordinated, we're probably appreciating how the *motion* of movement is flowing as the "coordinated" person does what they are doing. For example, watching ice skating competitions, one contestant's sense of *line* is clearer, more consistent throughout their routine. The sustained *line* testifies to the skater's sense of continuity, and the musicality of the skater.

Instead of showing *line* on my own body and asking students to imitate—which I knew was not a creative stimulus,—I thought of *line as locomotion:* a way of experiencing the parts of the whole body moving together as one, a whole-body experience, like walking or jumping. We *walk*, we *jump* with our whole body, we *slide*, and *turn* with our whole body, especially as children. All the other locomotive activities, such as twisting, hopping, leaping, swinging, etc., are permutations or combinations of these basic four locomotions: *walking, sliding, turning, jumping.*

To generate experiencing these locomotions, I spontaneously thought of 23 body parts that we can articulate separately: fingers (2), hands (4), elbows (6), shoulders (8), arms (10), neck (11), torso (12), waist (13), hip (15), legs (17), knees (19), ankles (21), toes (23). Five-year-olds have already naturally mastered how these parts are experienced together, while the fours are still working on it. They found it novel! Walk the fingers, walk the hands, walk the elbows, and so on down to the toes. No one ever asked them to think of walking fingers. They smiled. In the exercises, walking toes was an easy way to experience pointing to stretch the top of the feet; walking fingers out was a way to reach out to extend the hand, the arm. It was fun, for me as well! They weren't just imitating or translating a visual action into a physical event. It connected them to their own control, which

66

is always welcomed for our sense of independence and togetherness. They were implicitly reawakening their sensory experience, generating personal associations akin to Jeffrey's improvisation as *clay*.

SENSORY AWAKENING

I was unintentionally teaching the five-year-olds a perceptual awareness of what gets learned unconsciously by having them distinguish body parts to revive the *locomotion* experience. In so doing, the children were learning how to create an improvisational movement.

I started with *walking* parts and quickly realized that it was too exacting. The children tried, but it was troubling, uncomfortable. The joy disappeared from their faces. I quickly shifted to *sliding* each of the 23 articulated body parts. It was obviously so much easier! Walking parts took them away from the body as play. Sliding relaxed the muscles of their faces; their smiles reappeared. They slid the hand, had no trouble sliding the elbow, the shoulder. They had already mastered visualizing their skeletal body. Sliding parts was new, fun. It appealed to a playful *creative inner self*. For the five-year-olds, the idea of texture played a comparable *creative inner self* to the *textural* quality of the shapes six- and seven-year-olds made while exploring *clay*.

I wasn't yet aware of flow "through the muscles" at that time, which became central to my teaching many years later. I was focused on the educational aim in keeping with my conceptual model, *form and qualities, clay and locomotion.*

But I was still too intellectually driven. Tactile flow is a more perceptually sophisticated sensory awareness, a more emotionally laden experience.

I was pleased to find a focus that engaged the children's imagination in an age-appropriate way. The physical activities and the ideas dovetailed. The five-year-olds continued to explore sliding parts of the body, sliding from one part then another, evoking a continuity. They created their imagined environment just as Jeff created his imagined jungle and tiger. The continuity evoked self-metaphors: *I felt like a snake; I felt like lapping water on the sand, sliding back into the ocean; I was a seed growing out of the earth*; and many more that I don't recall as I write. These exploratory foci reawakened the mental with the sensory, strengthening a creative sensibility, a more conscious level of experience. To reinforce the physical with the visual, I had them draw on sheets of paper as they observed each other's individual improvisation. The excitement among them and towards me was intoxicating.

A few of the girls competed to sit next to me every Friday. It was wonderful to feel their love without any reservations. It took me many years to recognize how much I loved and missed this. Teaching movement explorations was tapping into the fountain of the children's love.

Their pride in their bodies' facility in naturally expressing images enhanced a self-validating excitement. Every child had a favorite locomotion in keeping with each child's embedded emotional developing sensibility. There were no postures or steps to follow.

All four *locomotions* were explored through improvisation during the two 18-week terms, from fall to summer. Towards the end of the spring term, I asked them to shift, if they wanted to, from one locomotion to another, whenever they wished to do so. They spontaneously found a way to flow from one to another.

I found this to be incredibly successful. The "23 parts" locomotion helped them to distinguish the differences in moving from one part to another. It accentuated a more conscious experiential sense of each locomotion, in the same way that each image generated a distinct sense of muscular variation for the six- to eight-year-olds in the *clay exercise*.

The locomotion that fit with girls' forming personalities shaped their hopes for the future. It was comparable to the way that six- to eight-year-olds had a favorite improvisational image, expressing how they felt the muscularity of their emotional selves. The smoothness of *sliding* for the girls who had chosen charm as important to them; *jumping* for the ones who had chosen assertiveness; *turning* for the ones who wanted to be free-spirited ballerinas; *walking* for those who imagined becoming nurses, caretakers. Experience and choices, feeding our feeling of control, or "individuating" as Margaret Mahler,[31] an early researcher of the early psychological stages of development, named it.

My understanding of creative movement was reinforced: a self-revealing process transforming into art.

Once again, I was unconsciously finding ways for the children to rekindle the sensory aspect of *inner motion* expressed though their own bodies, reawakening the experience of *motion* that is so natural, unquestionable for all of us as infants and toddlers, only interrupted by moments of terror when the future is suspended by the stiffening body of fear. All of us learn how to control our bodies by lifting our legs and arms voluntarily, turning over in the crib or bed, and eventually sitting up. Kinetic control becomes a source of pride, leading to aims and wishes becoming our way of thinking.

---

31 Margaret Mahler, Austrian-American psychiatrist, psychoanalyst and pediatrician, developed the separation-individuation theory referring to the stages an infant's cognitive development of ego and sense of identity as separate from the mother.

I was unwittingly teaching the retrieval of the earlier kinesthetic sensibility, analogous to the mythological Phoenix rising from the ashes.

Sensation awakens the basic experience of touch as well as the infant's connection to the experience of feelings. Jeff's *clay* improvisation generated the threatening aggression of the tiger and how he managed to kill it, with his "knife"–his sharp mind dealing with his own aggression at age seven.

This observation of what works for one age group that doesn't for another led to my understanding that each age unconsciously develops a different age-appropriate sense of their bodies by the ways their emotions accommodate the complexity of family and developing friendships. My observations predicated the syllabus and curriculum for each age group, from age three to adulthood, modifying what gets affectively emphasized in the exercises and what foci gets affectively explored as improvisation. I was experientially becoming convinced of the *physical developmental aspect of emotional expression* for each age: the physical expression of emotions. Dance is a particular form with its own aesthetic language, facilitating the subtlety of feelings. This is especially true of creative movement with its focus on improvisation.

This understanding added immeasurably to the traditional aim of flexibility and strength as central to dance training. Even though muscles need to be stretched for flexibility and strengthen by contractions (shortening) and extension (lengthening), how you contextualize these aims alters for each age. Three-year-olds like to run, and spin, get slightly dizzy, fall with glee, only to rise again and repeat. It's like reincarnation, death and rebirth, the fun of stretching and the fun of stiffening, a quickness of moods. I characterized their relationship as exploring their physical MASS–spinning like a swirl of pudding and collapsing like a balloon as the air escapes. This on-and-off impulsive expression of feelings changes by age four, when control of aims and outcomes becomes more of a focus. I called it PARTS, because of the explorations of muscular strength inherent in the control of tightening into the skeletal connections; differentiating isotonic from isometric, as we may professionally call it. The fours are excited by their upper arm contractions, like body builders.

I brought in a piece of jungle gym equipment that I could attach to the wall and pull out when I wanted to use it. I would introduce it towards the end of each class, beginning with the four-year-olds. The jungle gym had rounded metal bars that a child could grab and swing themselves to reach the next bar on the top. I was always underneath for safety and support if needed. There were also bars going down, the vertical support of the jungle gym, forming a ladder which they would climb up and then jump down onto a mat, challenging their sense of and fear of heights. The apparatus also included hanging rings, and a trapeze—a wooden bar from the upper left side of the frame which they used to lift themselves while managing to place the bar under their knees to hang upside down. The four-year-olds adored testing their strength and hanging from their legs. I always had mats underneath the jungle gym, and I was underneath or next to it for safety and support, carefully watching. The fives continued to enjoy the same challenges. But what they so avidly enjoyed changed with the six-year-old group.

Ability to control is not only kinetically useful, but becomes a governing principle of what we need to do to be in charge of fear that can collapse our resourceful gains. Meeting new challenges is a source of being appreciated as well overcoming fear! I recall the four-year-olds being called "the negative fours," because they could assert such strong feelings: good-bad, strong-weak, I will-I won't, like-dislike and so on. They are tough, able to allow you in or shut you out.

Jean Piaget[32] pointed out that four-year-olds can consider something gone forever, forever lost, never to return. It's a powerful developmental, conscious realization that is at once frightening and provides an unburdening freedom from a binding attachment. This thinking ability helps children to deal with fear and recover from loss. The separation from the earlier all-encompassing Object/Mother, whose presence is survival, is also a shield against the pain and terror of abandonment, and shadows of unmitigated loneliness. This helps developmental stage helps us to deal with the ambivalence of whatever may come into play psychically. The not-uncommon resistance to the unconscious begins early and is often difficult to overcome and to accept as a natural part of our psychic life.

Understanding how each age and stage of development can be expressed through creative movement was my emotional universe. Teaching for me was like walking barefoot on grass, reviving sensations forgotten on the sidewalks of ambition, expectations, and judgements.

I'm reminded that with the six-to-eight-year-olds, *clay* was the image with which I began, followed by *wire* as they neared seven, requiring a sustained malleable hardness, like a paper clip or copper wire that can be shaped. *Rubber band* required the ability to sense the motion of muscles lengthening and shortening as one moves; a more internal sensory self-experience that exploring being a *rubber band* facilitated. One boy, who became a professional ballet principle, told me after a concert in which he starred that he still used *rubber band* as his understanding of what the role needed from him physically. The exercises began to emphasize muscles to stretch and contract quickly.

---

32 Jean Piaget, Swiss psychologist and philosopher who systematically studied the cognitive development of children.

Piano, the image for soft, was the most difficult of all the images. Of the many, many images I tried, it had the most variation in terms of imagining the whole body as a frame affected by the sound of notes and chords. One girl, who became a professional artist as an adult, captured this complexity beautifully with her paintings and technical expertise: borders of objects and colors interacting delicately without confusing the edges of separate images. This takes skill and an impressive sensibility; she came from a sophisticated poetic and analytic family.

I strongly identified with this stage of emotional development, changes with a sense of cohesiveness, not unlike actors sustaining the fundamental element of a character throughout the changing intentions of scenes in the play. It helped me to understand how to work more thoughtfully and sensitively when directing actors.

Part of starting a school—which I viewed as an institution—to educate children and adults in Creative Movement was to have an overarching curriculum, to be clear where one starts, and how one develops, into a certifiable professional. At the same time, I was intellectually and creatively transforming the mean-spirited *"never love with the same passion ever again"* mindset. I was opening up to ambivalence, to the subtlety of feelings and their quicksilver potential.

The immersion in creative movement teaching had taken over my insular, private-oriented passion. This larger frame opened the suffocating claustrophobic infantile universe of terror and love. A universe that is both grand and terrifying.

CURRICULUM

My revelation with Jeff's *clay* improvisation gave me the sense of discovering the fundamental basis for teaching creative movement, namely, *how the student experiences their body*. It wasn't hard to consider this fundamental idea in relationship with what I understood constitutes all dance; namely *line, form, qualities* (variations of muscle tone), *space*, and *time*. I believed at the time that I had creatively resolved *line, form, and qualities*. The curriculum for three and four was equally framed. although not as distinctively. The younger ages still tended to act out sudden impulses, appearing/disappearing like thunder and lightning. A creative activity I recall observing was the four-year-olds running to the teacher's drum beat and freezing all of their body *Parts* into a statue when the drum stopped. The differences in the individual shapes were remarkable to observe: arms, heads. torsos, legs turned to stone as if by the magic wand of the Ice Queen in *The Chronicles of Narnia* stories.[33] An example of how quickly they could physically transform.

Three-year-olds could not stop as dramatically because their physical *Mass* was caught up in the *Motion* of running, so it took them longer to bring the *Mass* into a held posture. The power of sensation, the *motion* of feeling was still stronger than the mental directive to

---

33 *The Chronicles of Narnia*, a series of seven fantasy novels for children by C. S. Lewis, 1950-56.

control. Their feelings need our patient sensitivity, despite the fact that they already show social and intellectual skills. The ability to freeze for the fours characterizes their capacity for discipline, emotional obstinacy, or total repression or remembering and never forgetting.

In my recovery from Covid, I kept trying to pinpoint whether I was four or five when I had an asthma attack in Cuba. It was a one-time event; I never had another. Writing about the fours gives me the sense of probably being four. I was frozen in an emotional posture. I didn't seem to have any other way of saying that I was suffocating over what was going on externally at home or internally in my psyche. My parents rushed me to the Casa de Socorro,[34] *the emergency facility at the hospital in Havana. Breathing issues would show up as I aged, corresponding to repressed emotional issues throughout my life.*

The fours need our indulgent perspective as adults for their unyielding behavior. We need to be patient and consider the underlying terror; they are protecting themselves from: separation, shame, desire, guilt, punishment. It's a lot to process. I hope you agree.

I should mention that every class was structured for the initial *kinesthetic* exercises, followed by exploratory improvisational foci emphasizing spontaneous *sensory* movement, and ending with the jungle gym for pure, exuberant *kinetic* activity.[35] This covered what I considered the three basic aspects in the development of movement for the children.

My next curricular challenge was to discover a creative approach for exploring *space* and *time* in keeping with my Conceptual Model.

---

34 La Casa de Socorro, in Spanish, means The House of Help.

35 Kinesthetic: a person's awareness, via the sensory organs, of movement of parts of the body. Sensory: what is perceived by the five senses. Kinetic: that which results from, or is related to, motion.

MY UNFORGETTABLE AWAKENING

At the American Dance Festival at Connecticut College during the summer of 1957, I shared a room with Aryeh Kalev,[36] an Israeli. I still spoke Hebrew fluently at the time, so the dialogue between us, including his English which was more than good enough, was easy. He was attending the ADF with a scholarship grant that continued for six months of study at the Graham school. His wife and young daughters were in Ramat Gan, a lovely suburb of Tel Aviv, where he had founded a successful creative movement school. His age never came up, but he was clearly older, quieter, and not caught up in changing me. I wasn't afraid. I discovered that he came from Czechoslovakia, where his parents once had a department store. When Hitler managed to annex the German-speaking part of Czechoslovakia, he was sent to Palestine through the Youth Aliyah, an organization set up to save the Jewish children of Europe during the Third Reich. He grew up in a kibbutz rich enough to sponsor his studies in Swiss gymnastics when he was older.

I'm recalling Aryeh's story of sitting at a tennis match, when he was approached by a man seated somewhere behind him who asked him if he was from Czechoslovakia, then pinpointed the specific region

---

36 Aryeh Kalev created his own unique dance and choreography teaching method.

that the family came from. The man's astute observations surprised him. The man introduced himself as the originator of a skeletal and facial system developed over many years. Aryeh had also studied yoga. He related to the man of having seen a film of a 150-year-old yogi who was able to twist his legs behind his neck. Aryeh was clearly more involved than I was with the varied physical and spiritual dimensions of movement as an expression of the psyche; beyond my subjectively driven interest in movement as a way to vent bottled-up feelings.

One particular morning, I returned to our room, upset by something that had happened during the morning technique classes. Noting my anxiety, Aryeh asked if I would like to try a relaxation technique. I consented.

He spread the Army blanket from his bed and folded it to cushion my back. My legs were spread equidistant from the groin, arms stiff, a thumb distance from the thighs. His instructions, slowly and quietly voiced, placed my head vertically and horizontally at the center of the back of my skull. The center felt markedly different from where I usually imaged as my center. Just those simple actions made me more conscious of my sensory experience of the body than ever before. To reinforce the center on a sensory level, he asked me to turn my head just a little to the right, then slowly and quietly return it to my newly established center. I did this to the left as well, repeating the process several times until the newly sensed centerpoint on the back of my head felt unquestionable.

Since I wasn't ever used to moving so slowly—which Aryeh observed—he continued slowly asking me to imagine drawing a line down my neck to the right shoulder and redrawing the line back to the center. As you might have already anticipated, imagining these lines went on through the whole body, palms, fingers, feet and toes. Because my shoulders were already rounded forward, I couldn't place

80

my palms flat on the floor. I was amazed by my distorted misalignment at just 23.

My inability to place my palms flat helped me to acknowledge how unconsciously body misalignments develop. I began to relax. After having me draw lines from the back of the head center to the toes, and then simultaneously through the whole body, he then asked me to focus on the breath: detailing how it enters through the nostrils continues through the front and top of the skull, descending the back of the spine, filling the lungs, then exhaling through the mouth.

Observing the slow, quiet involuntary process of the breath was eye-opening. Such a defined breathing process was totally new to me.

We stayed with this for a time. Suddenly, my chest began to heave sobs without any tears. This went on uncontrollably for a few short minutes. I was totally arrested by the experience of the body revealing unintended emotions on a totally somatic level.

It was remarkable that the body could speak and cry without shedding tears. Our bodies have distinct memories of the original events that our minds have unconsciously pushed aside, unavailable for articulating.

I laid there quietly recovering before he asked to turn on my side and bring the knees in towards the chest in order to roll on them to stand. *I had lost a sense of time. I felt my arms longer, standing taller.*

We needed to go to lunch. Walking out of the room, I had a sensory experience so unusual that my chest came alive just now as I recall the sensations. There was a sense of space startlingly new to me when it happened; a weightlessness while walking—not quite suspended, but an incredible lightness of being, in every step. This was followed by a sudden appreciation of the geometry of buildings and pathways, as if viewed by the architect's aesthetic, creative eye. It continued for several hours as we sat down to lunch. The uncanny sense remained, so different from my usual sense of space, which

I usually defined by directions or objects, such as close or faraway, or the reasons why the buildings were grouped together. This *inner* awareness and sense of space lasted for several hours, and forever in my psychic life.

Space as what we live In. It was more than the external outside! I was acknowledging the sensory experience of being a part of space. This was clearly in contrast to my usual generalized thinking: *of course everything exists in space,* the sensory as distinguished from the conceptual.

In retrospect, I lived in my wishes, their fulfillment or failure. This may be hard to consider unless you've experienced this distinction. The distinction has never left me, even though the heightened sensory awareness eventually dissipated as I involuntarily returned to my habitual thinking. The integration of the sensory with my thinking continues into my 90th year. The integrative process of analysis, to quote Freud, is interminable.[37]

This brings to mind a time, years later, when a few parents asked me to start a class for their teenage daughters. It was a small class of 14-year-olds. I began as usual with the initial exercises, then decided to introduce my space experience with Aryeh.

I had them lay down on their backs, center their heads, secure the imagined point on the back of the head. I gave them directions in an almost a monotone voice, to lessen the power of suggestion (of which I was becoming more therapeutically aware); continuing with visualizing a line from the sensed point of the back of the skull through the neck, then slowly descending from the shoulder down the upper arm, past the elbow through the forearm, past the wrist and

---

37 "Analysis Terminable and Interminable," S. Freud, 1937.

the fingertip pads, touching the floor to sense the line going through the tips of each finger.

My pacing slowed, relaxing the mind unnoticed. Eventually, through the tips of toes with the imagined lines passing through as with the fingertips. I shortened the exercise to a minimum of 40 minutes, to leave enough time for their movement improvisations.

One particular girl still stands out in my mind. Her improvisation began with tiny wriggles through the whole body, then very slowly struggling to stand, opening her arms like a large bird into flight. I asked her to share what had happened for her. She responded, "I was a snake moving around, shedding my skin slowly, changing into a bird in flight." Her story line reminded me of Jeff and the *clay*. It was obvious from the way she spoke that she was totally aware that it all happened like a dream. It reminded me of the Guatemalan Quetzal bird[38] worshiped by Mayans and Aztecs. On an age-appropriate level, it possibly expressed her struggle in becoming the wished-for free adult.

Since the girl's father was a psychoanalyst, her awareness of mythology might have had a more personal family connection, which I did not explore in a creative movement class. This was in the late 1960s, way before my analytic training.

Awareness happens in so many ways over one's lifetime. Systems conceptualize the personal process exquisitely, like the stitching of needlepoint.

I felt that I had found the beginning of a creative movement foci for exploring space. But it required a capacity for a listening process, in contrast with the more direct physical foci discoveries I had developed earlier.

---

38 The Quetzal was **symbol of freedom,** because it was believed that it preferred to die of hunger rather than to live as a prisoner.

ADOLESCENCE

Let me take a step back. The nine-to-12-year-olds were not prepared emotionally for a passive, internally focused exploration. It didn't engage their interest. This age group was clearly, from my perspective, focused on *kinetic* excellence. Their explorations of the earlier work with *locomotion* and *images,* as creative explorations to catch them up on the inner sense of the two basic sensibilities of *line and form,* *were* half-hearted. They seemed more self-conscious than the younger students, concerned with how their classmates were looking at them. Self-judgment was apparent to me in the way they exercised, pushing for flexibility and by how far into space and how quickly their stretch could reach. The speed of the adolescent's imagination towards a self-identity seemed apparent to me.

This shift to space, to time away from mastering the body *mass* had been going on since moving lips, turning, sitting up, standing, walking, changing infancy into toddlerhood, and early childhood; the evidence was incontrovertible. Pride and determination can inadvertently lead to bad physical habits. It is a process of mind/body that unconsciously displaces the earlier body/mind/spirit togetherness of infancy, toddlerhood and childhood with a strong sense of *intent.* The dynamic connection between body and sensation was being slowly subdued by *intentionality.* Competitiveness and authority were driving the nine-to 12s, albeit apprehensively expressed. They needed to be protected without limiting their burgeoning energy.

I discussed my thoughts about this age group with Lyn Pyle, a principal teacher with a Masters Degree in Comparative Literature, and a founder of Mass Transit Street Theater.[39] This sparked her idea for the perfect "protective cover" for the students in the face of those powerful forces of competitiveness and self-consciousness: *Sheets!*

We gave each student a fabric sheet to lie underneath while they explored *locomotion* and *Images,* protecting them from their self-consciousness and facilitating their earlier metaphoric imagination in safety. It was amazing how they took to this simple act of hiding under sheets.

The ballet barre became a part of the exercises because of their focus on self-definition. Limbs were treated with a power and a meaning of their own, not unlike their four-year-old self, albeit with the older students' sharpened awareness of their socially revealing implications…the understated seriousness of adolescence, whose social realities occupy so much of their inner and outer life.

Sheets remained a viable approach for the ten-to-12s, who used them as capes to be thrown about, shared or discarded, like the chrysalis of butterflies. The sheets provided their intuitive impulses with an external cover for creative expression. The self-assertiveness of young ladies in the making seemed obvious to me.

Although it was using a practical external element—*Sheets* to liberate the inner process, their fantasy self—it wasn't a focus that elicited improvisation of the *inner motion of unconscious associations,* like Jeffrey's waking dream.

It is only as of this writing that I question the solution of *Sheets.* Sheets did not promote a *sensory* cohesion of mind/body/spirit.

---

39 Mass Transit Street Theater, founded in 1970, is a Bronx-based performance company known nationally for storytelling, spoken word, music and dance.

The sheets liberated the girls' impulses, a way to express freedom, conflicts, determination, without eliciting their inner unconscious associations. I suspect Lyn asked for their associations, but I wonder if any of the girls experienced a story as they explored *locomotion* or the *images* under the sheets. I may be doing Lyn an injustice in not remembering.

I have tried to demonstrate how my teaching has been healing my repression of loss and anger. Jeff's clay and my analysis of its value began an awakening to the internal unconscious associations and how they are represented as in dreams, then altering on the path of self-control into an awareness of how it could stay connected to the earlier stages of sensory experiential relatedness.

These physical explorations were central to both creative teaching and my theater work. Metaphors, stories surfacing from inside the person's own experience.

My sensuality and sexual imagination flourished during this period, affecting my focus. My moral balance hinged on the practicalities of family, business, and pedagogic explorations. The intellectual, however, could be sabotaged by split-off erotic sensations, triggering unresolved, unconscious longings.

A conscious sense of anxiety came into my awareness as past love and desire resurfaced. Physical symptoms appeared over several months: armpit rashes, an unusual stiff neck needing treatment, a buttock muscle frozen regardless of whether I stood, sat, or laid down. I was always in pain. The symptoms lasted for months, regardless of a variety of treatments.

I also recall having a roving eye, like a lonely sailor perched high up on the mast on the lookout for land or enemy ships. The sea reminds me of my mother, who thought of herself as a rowboat tossed about on a stormy sea. There was sense of constant danger. I was as self-

conscious as the nine-to-12-year-olds. In retrospect, I was more scared than I realized.

BOUNDARIES

My boundaries were tested by my first evening adult class. Like all professional classes, it was structured by exercises, followed by across-the-floor dance phrases. I recall a scissor step pattern common in folk dances—step right, cross left leg behind, step right, rest, then repeat to the other side, with arm gestures. Or the more common running pattern: one, two, three, leap, crossing on the diagonal of the studio. But more central to what was coming into focus for me were rounded shoulders, stiffened spines, legs, and smells inviting repulsion in one case and attraction in others. I stopped touching bodies to have them sense what I mentioned they should pay attention to.

I cite the adult dance class to convey how my unexamined erotism had impacted my unconscious reactions to the nine-to-12-year-olds, which contributed to my delight in *Sheets* as the solution. This was obviously a reminder of what happened fortuitously in the class with the 14-year-old girl who imagined a skin-shedding snake. Both Jeff of the *clay* improvisation and the 14-year-old suggested an openness to their guarded imaginations, freed from the boundaries of family sexual and aggressive values. Freed. I regret not thinking of this *coming out of* aspect, for the nine-to-12-year-old group, because of my suppressed fantasies, which I unconsciously and conveniently treated as self-consciousness, but could not explore because of my own inhibiting family standards.

My creative explorations were stifled by an unnamed anxiety. *I had so much more to process emotionally.*

The practical—so often covered in artistry—was draped over my anxiety against underlying feelings too powerful to harness. It makes me think of Icarus[40] who, because of his immaturity, defied his father Daedalus' advice not to fly too high into the sun with the wings his father fashioned from birds' feathers and wax to allow them to escape their imprisonment in King Minos' tower. The wax melted, and Icarus fell into the sea, where he drowned.

Unbound freedom has its dangers as we age. The energy of the call to freedom also cloaks anxiety's underlying traumatic fear.

I pulled back the cloak that covered my hidden self by simplifying across-the-floor dance phrases for the adult classes into a practical physical consideration. "Just swing the arm to the right, then swing the other arm to the left. Don't worry about the steps. Let your feet move automatically in response to the swing of your arms with the music."

By dropping the responsibility to co-ordinate the arms and legs, the students were free from the burden of memory, and of not having to follow my demonstrated instructions, as the music helped them just swing. This is closer to psychodynamic therapy, which gives the patient the emotional space to simply associate. It was an early approach to addressing individual movement association, pursued years later in an advanced class.

I could see that these adults were relieved not to have to satisfy the specifics of a pattern of steps. Consider how embedded in most of us since infancy is the habitual impulse to follow emotional patterns.

---

40 Icarus, a minor character in Greek mythology who did not survive the transition from boyhood to adulthood.

Asking the adults to just swing an arm registered as *Free at Last,* if I may borrow that allusion. It also changed their implicit thinking about me as an authority they must follow like a parent, which is both explicit and implicit in dance classes. This psychological consideration was not conscious at the time. My playful seductiveness made classes fun.

I transformed my hidden seducing proclivity by the following three elements:

1. Breathing

I asked the students to just sense breathing in and out while they ran around the studio to music; liberating the sheer freedom of motion without any particular focus. "Just be aware of your breath as you move."

The breath changes involuntarily with every emotion, whether unconscious or conscious, and with every action, as we have all experienced when we rush. Breathing problems may be indicative of underlying emotional issues; a psychological consideration I was not making at the time, as my focus was on the freedom of movement. Although the students were free not to follow steps, it became quite clear to me that they tended to forget about inhaling and exhaling by settling into the musical accented measure. The need for boundaries, for safety, was stronger than their own breath.

The focus on breathing affected the unconscious relational boundary by subduing the pressured aim of the movement activity. It's like doing a two-step timing to a foxtrot so that your partner won't feel rushed, feels safe, taken care of! The interpersonal consideration is the partner, not the music. Feeling safe applied to the tendency to follow the musical measure of a fox trot or a waltz; timing as safety while losing the awareness of the body. From a psychological point of view, it's like fitting into the family without a voice, without the feelings of the self, just to feel safe.

I was teaching about the energy of feeling to which jazz musicians are attuned, and that orchestra conductors rehearse avidly. Every musician in a jazz combo registers—senses—the feeling being expressed, and responds to it with a dialogue of improvisation, going along with the feeling or cooling it. Since I used my bodily experience at the time as a register of feeling, I would demonstrate the energy, the tempo, the *spirit* of the music. I would vocally encourage the students to vary the timing of inhaling/exhaling, to have some conscious control in how their breathing was impacted by running to feel in sync with the music. The repetition of this awareness with a variety of music continued for a number of classes. When they got used to how they could change their breath and the run in relationship to the music, they could then differentiate the habitual "settling in" tendency from the tempo, the energy. They could then simply stand still, not move, and yet continue to stay alive to the tempo, their bodily experience of it. Some people do this without ever being conscious of their inborn musical, sensory improvisations. Dance auditions, especially for summer stock, follow this standard—although they may not word it as I do—to choose who stays and who is quickly thanked and let go off.

It was difficult to move the adults out their habitual, embedded pattern of this self-protective approach to fit into the downbeat, the measure. They could recognize it in others, but learning to apply it to themselves took awhile. It became obvious that their resistance was psychological, without my naming it as such. Engaging the interplay between the body and acknowledging emotional associations is one of the values of individual in-depth therapy.

Safety, security is an emotional need for an infant. Their whole sensory system is programmed for that need. Babies are inherently reactive to every stimulus. The integration of stimuli is hard work, so they need to sleep a lot, as every parent discovers. Infants are the air, the sound, the. music, the thunder, the vibration; they are the universe. They are by nature a part of everything. They are connected to the sound of speech while *in utero*. The mother or mother substitute is the rudder, the sail of the boat in the sea of life.

Security remains a fundamental psychic need throughout our lives. Too many stimuli cause an inner tremor, a sensation we later call fear. When the infant is overwhelmed by the universe, the suddenness affects the musculature around the diaphragm, a suffocating moment effecting the flow of blood to the brain. If it lasts too long, a lifelong self-protective system becomes a part of our character. The natural flow of feelings goes awry, and the sensation of motion is fraught with tension.

This happened for me after my Covid experience, which I will address later.

Exploring the primacy of the breath went a long way towards recovering a more open sense of self. I could see the embedded tensions relaxing, arms becoming looser as the students ran to the music. A less guarded individuality began to come through. To make sure that everyone was experiencing this primacy, I would vary the music to reinforce their ability to respond to the energy of different pieces of music. I would spend many classes on fostering this sensitivity, impacting the way they looked at each other moving. Individuality became more conscious.

Affecting those tensions is what reclaiming love is all about. And the physical process dictated my explorations and my insights, continually bringing me closer to the calm of the love I sought.

2. *Motion: the inner sensory awareness of movement*

I equated *Motion* with imagination, an aspect of mind that just seems to flow out of us.

I explored the sensation quite literally like a children's game that just came to mind, by asking everyone to form a circle and face counterclockwise, with the inside arm pointing to the middle of the floor of the circle, while the outside arm was lifted up away from the center, tilting the whole body and eyes towards the center of the circle. Then, walking slowly counterclockwise into an increasing pace to a slight run, they were to sustain the body slant until it affected their balance, as if falling into the middle of the circle.

Noticing the disorientation, I asked quickly for them to stop and reestablish their balance. After a few seconds observing their recovery, I shared my thinking about how motion might be handled without having stop to recover their sense of safety.

"Would you return slowly into the slight run by moving away from the circle when you sense the disorientation, and past the sensation of motion through your own body as quickly as you can."

Freed from the responsibility of maintaining the group, the circle allowed each person to process the *continuity of motion,* however it happened for each one of them. They had to do this a few times in order not to smooth out the transition. They were now in control of the *continuity of motion* without having to freeze for safety against their fear, and the conscious or unconscious social responsibility to the group.

They understood the difference between their personal *experience of motion* inherent in *movement*. The simple repetition of this distinction opened up their capacity to improvise, altering the *fear* of movement as potentially dangerous to become stabilized by keeping time. *Dancing was not basically a skill to be mastered but intrinsically an expression of our sensory experience.* Improvisation became more fun.

Individuality was implicitly bolstered until their experience of *Motion* could be sustained without cutting it off for the safety of balance. The continuity of balance became implicit in how it is passed through the various parts of the body.

Consider this process as the essence of DANCE!

It strikes me, as I write, that my inventive explorative choice was an unconscious turning the clock back to being a three-year-old, as I previously described. By age four, I was seldom physically quiet. It wasn't easy for my mother to get me to go to sleep. An oppositional element became entrenched into my character without intent, eventually to be analytically worked through with great difficulty over many years.

Motion as the free flow of fantasy; it was a physical sensory experience the class could tap into. It belonged to them, movement as freedom of mind as well as body—the implicit value of *creative movement.*

This was an imaginative way to have the students experience what dancers seem to develop unconsciously. A lot of people like to dance, but what makes a *dancer* is a sense of physical freedom with music or with metaphors; when a twist of the torso is expressive of turning away from someone or something. Choreographers naturally have this sensibility, which they may or may not ever question consciously. They have to dance their inner sensory emotional experience, regardless of how they conceptualize or word it.

I was discovering and proving that the inner sensory world of creative movement can be taught; a non-verbal communication of what is felt unconsciously.

By exploring the elements of dance, I was freeing myself from the rage of failed love, of abandonment, of entrapment.

In retrospect, I didn't consider how my students were internalizing the sensation of *Motion*. How they handling their feelings was not my focus at the time. I just observed, and trusted my observational sense that one person sensed the *Motion* more easily while another appeared to be doing it more mechanically. Over a decade later, I discovered from a totally different perspective how to help everyone experience *Motion* more fully, without having to experience imbalance, which is frightening.

As usual, I combined *Breath* with *Motion* so the students could experience how they worked together. Dancers do this "naturally." You can see it in their phrasing of the choreography. You may see it more clearly with one dancer than another.

We may also hear this distinction when a person speaks. The subtlety of phrasing differentiates one actor from another. This distinction is always more than craft.

3. Beat: the most conscious element of movement

Beat is a unit in music, a measure of time. You can think of rhythms as the timing element of emotions. The metronome is what a piano teacher uses to have the student experience the regularity of the *Beat*. I did the same with *Beat* physically. I had the adults stamp their feet: one, one, one, one, endlessly, right, left, right, left, then with music with an obvious beat, in keeping with the stamping of our feet. The comparison seemed totally clear to everyone.

I followed this up with keeping the *Beat* with just the knees, then only the hips, all the way up the body until they just moved the thumbs, then only the tongue, then not move at all. The sudden "not move" made them realize how the mind holds onto the repetition of the beat.

Beat is memory! Time is memory! Time is a construct of memory. The logic of what I was saying also seemed clear to everyone as they experienced it physically.

Beat made an incredible impact on the students' freedom to improvise. The beat can be kept by any part of the body, and moved around in whatever way it occurs to each person. This is exactly how the five-year-olds were able to use the *23 parts of the body.*

I continued the exercise with different kinds of music to help them sense that there is always a beat to every musical score. When they sensed the beat internally, even when not moving, it facilitated their playfulness while improvising. They could more consciously hear the accenting of a beat, or the resting of a beat, or the doubling of the beat, and find a way to play with the beat. This elicited a recognition of unconscious impulses, unconscious wishes inherent in playing with *Beat.*

These associations and physical experiences were exactly what I hoped for; a way of personally owning the *Beat.* An internalization of it, giving life to a word, a measure of feeling.

As usual, I combined *Beat* with *Breath* to relax the tight mental focus that some students box themselves into when making sure not to lose the *Beat.* The *Breath* is used in all physical disciplines like Yoga for exactly this reason: to loosen the tightness of memory as control. I also combined *Beat* with *Motion* to accentuate the flow of the *Beat.* You can hear these distinctions in the drumming of a rock or jazz piece, or in a piece of classical music. It dictates the way a song is scored. It distinguishes one concert instrumentalist from another with exactly the same music. It allows us to listen to the person, to what they are feeling as an artist, as a person.

Exploring each focus separately is academic. In dance, they work together, although choreographers will tend to emphasize one more than another. Treating them as totally distinct was helpful for reexperiencing them with a new awareness. Verbal therapy pursues associations in a similar way by staying close to the patient's process to reveal what is hidden. I sensed the parallel in the disciplines—distinct frameworks addressing the same internal primary process.

These three exploratory foci, *Breath, Motion, and Beat,* constituted the beginner's syllabus I explored over two years. It took time to re-experience how these elements seemed so easily taken in as children.

Breath relaxes the muscular tension of *attention* that builds-up unconsciously in the musculature, awakening a natural capacity to physically move to the energy of what the dance is sensing.

Motion equates with an inner sensation that often triggers imagination. If and when it does, the gulf between mind and body narrows. The sensate arousal is a more kinesthetic response to what the dancer is hearing. It corresponds to an inner sensory voice that can be articulated.

Beat grounds by organizing, as a way to deal with all music. The students' ability to play flowers without thinking, diminishing self-consciousness. All of these aspects are mutually inclusive and were eventually combined.

It was obviously easier for some people than others, because each of these three elements is so profoundly conditioned during infancy and toddlerhood. My own psychoanalytic experience eventually dovetailed with my understanding of what movement teaching revealed to me.

I am still struck seeing a toddler practically running to keep up with the parent holding the child's hand while rushing to get wherever she/he is determined to get to, expecting the toddler to keep up with her/his haste. Is it any wonder that the child will experience the parent as impatient, determined, self-assertive, demanding? These are early in life conditioning experiences. *Breath, Motion, and Beat* explorations bring these embodied elements into a potentially conscious perceptual associative aliveness.

I never combined this process with verbal therapy. I kept them separate in my mind; the private from the external, just as love is different from attraction. It took me a long time to understand this distinction.

Like all awareness, the movement explorations liberate us out of the claustrophobic darkness of control. They open us up to our personal character habits that can rob us of our creative, adaptive capacity.

The freedom with which these aspects loom large in our development has a great deal to do with the professional choices we make. It helps us to live more openly in all we do.

All of what was happening arose out of my sensitivity to the tensions of self-consciousness. As I became more involved with psychoanalytic therapy, I equated these tensions with repressed feelings. It made sense because it had become obvious to me that the mind uses the body as a substitute for feelings. The body registers feelings through sensations, expressed through behavior: the quickness or reticence of how we do things, or interact with ourselves or others. Becoming alive to these bodily sensory symptoms affected my own history with emotional repression. It wasn't easy.

Teaching remained central to my own awakening to self and love.

What I was doing with the adults is what happened with the children. Adults are free to act on their sensations. The only limits are, is it appropriate? is it acceptable? And even those considerations of social right and wrong are too often crossed, because the felt sensation can be overwhelming. The conscious perception of *sensation* was the focus to bring to awareness. From a movement point of view, the perceptual sensitivity of touch, of the feet to the floor, was the most available and irrefutable. There is no need for imagination. It is totally rational and easy to teach. (I will deal later with how the change in the exercises was affected by this understanding.)

I was however still entrenched in my theoretical formulation as to what constitutes all dance training: *line, form, qualities* (muscular variations), *space and time.* Creative techniques for exploring these elements are conceptual; in essence, metaphors, an appeal to our intellectual sense of structure, a framework that holds things together. The personal relationship between structure and imagination in movement is a private emotional journey of awareness, not an emotionally simple or lighthearted journey.

I have come to view these understandings through my analysis as psychologically related to intellectual seductions engaging my adult students with excitement and playfulness. I needed to get older and wiser to give up the weight of this intellectual and playful container.

SPACE

Space was the next category in my conceptual model to explore. In my dance training, space was defined by directions.

1. Directions

There are nine directions: front, back, side, diagonal, up, down, in, out, around. I explored each one by suggesting imaging the front of their body: face, chest, torso, front of the pelvis, thighs, sheens, down to the ankles, walking then into a faster pace run around the studio with music while imaging only the front of the body. I referenced it as "presentational" theater, like children's theater directed towards the audience, or as Shakespeare had an actor talk directly to the audience, sharing private thoughts about what is going on in the play, inviting the audience into the action, a technique known as "breaking the fourth wall." The contrast is "representational" theater where the action stays on stage, behind the curtain (the fourth wall).

I continued this approach with all the directions, alluding to theatrical, literary or dance analogies. For example, the Limόn dance technique is a broadened upper chest focus, up and out, accentuated by the Humphrey/Weidman polarity of Fall and Recovery theory; the upper sternum lift in Cecchetti Ballet technique is usually up and in. The polarity in all ballet technique is plié/ballon; Bournonville ballet technique, grounded in its folk-dance tradition, of quick foot work is *down to up*, akin to Merce Cunningham's approach to his technique.

Modern Dance's distinctive explorations were the use of the floor and horizontal planes *down and out;* Martha Graham's *contraction/release* focus is *in to out;* Cunningham, a former principal dancer with the Graham company liberated the bind on emotionally driven shapes and gestures that powerfully characterized so much of Modern Dance as choreographers refocused on chance interactions challenging speed, balance, and sharp stops. This was *out and out.* Every choreographer could be characterized by the use of directions. Time-*the present, the now*-was an inescapable consequence of World War II dealing with the ever-present life-and-death reality. It was *out* without apology! These associations contextualized my characterizations of these dance styles and techniques, personal character and cultural changes.

My intention with *Directions* was to build *Form* by experiencing the total shape of the body, to give their improvisations a more complete physicality. Adults could recognize their habituated chosen direction, the unconsciously embodied aspect of themselves. It was my own awakening to the psychological defenses. Denial is *out;* the inner feeling is denied and projected *out: It's not me, it's them.* I was paralleling creative movement with psychoanalytic understandings.

I was delighted by the way I framed these associations intellectually. But when I looked at the students' improvisations, I didn't see much change. Were they deluding themselves imagining the explorative elements I presented? Was I deluding myself by my rationally bound associations? We can treat thought as magical. "I think therefore I am," said the French philosopher René Descartes,[41] the father of

---

41 Descartes (1596-1860), in addition to being a philosopher, was also a scientist and mathematician.

rationalism. It is only at present that I can admit to the rationalizing of my early thinking to encourage the internal creative process.

2. Intuition: an aspect of an inner experience

The subtle embodied expression of feeling that always moved me was still my private guiding standard. This brings to mind the Yiddish word my mother often used, *mitgefil*, to feel with. I was teaching the way in which this subtle aspect of self appears through our physical sensory awakening.

At one point, in an effort to encourage their own sensory impulses, I suggested, "Think of your breath as a gesture; inhaling as a gesture, exhaling as a gesture." It was an unusual suggestion. Each motion, small or large, is a gesture. It evoked a powerful self-observing awareness of every aspect of motion for individuals who were already celebrated for their self-observing abilities. It fascinated the students in a never-before-considered experience. It may read as stifling, but the novelty of the suggestion overcame everyone's apprehension. Something truly new was taking place, not to be dismissed. It was an awareness they had never experienced in the way I was suggesting. It slowed down every movement, eliciting the emotional quality of an inner intention. Something was coming through that was a surprise to me.

The avant-garde theater director and playwright Robert Wilson employed this slowing-down process to heighten the audience's awareness of the details of an action. The slowed-down action is so startling that the emotional affect comes into consciousness.

As you might imagine, this little experiment could not last long, given the usual connection to movement as freedom, instinct, impulse, release. It did elicit a more embodied quality to every gesture. This embodied quality registered for me as *weight,* in the sense of a more relaxed mass to every movement. I experienced the presence of the students' bodies in the same way we observe toddlers mastering walking between 12 and 18 months. The jerky movements of babyhood by the not-yet-developed musculature are gone. The child's instinctual feelings become more kinetically habituated. The connection between whatever was happening emotionally came through their movement. But invariably, toddlers settle into rhythmic patterns dissociated from the embodied feeling of babyhood and toddlerhood. The *wishing* aspect becomes stronger, more dominant than the sensory experience. Wishing becomes equated with feeling, as if they were synonyms.

I recall asking adults to allow a sudden vibration in a hand or body part to happen. I don't recall that it was affective. Their movement remained intentional. The awareness of the unconsciously manifest *inner motion* that vibrations express wasn't clear to them by the way I spoke about it.

I was frustrated. I gave up on those sorts of explorative suggestions. Students needed to feel gratified by what they were learning. I was not strictly an academic institution, I wasn't establishing a binding cult, and keeping students was essential to making a living. This rationale began to change unwittingly because individual sessions dealing with misalignment issues were also happening.

3. Misalignments: muscles and bones

To facilitate the end of the exercise portion of the class, I used a spring through the legs into jumping—a standard ending of exercise in all the modern and ballet classes I had taken, which crowns the energy generated by the effort, pressure, anticipation, determination of exercising.

I defined for the students a line on the sole of the feet, running from the heel to the 4th *toe*, the one next to the little toe. It's an alignment I sensed in my own feet while lifting the arch of the foot off the floor, through the ankle into the calve muscles. An aligned continuity from the floor through the musculature made possible my intention to jump.

The clarity of that alignment became my starting point, as something to sense at the beginning of the exercises. It was startling to realize how problematic this was for some of the students. Sensing so specific a line of sensation from the heel to the 4th *toe* at the ball of the feet took them away from a more generalized, undefined contact with the floor, making the intention to jump into a willful act. I can call it magical thinking. They didn't argue with my explanation of how visualizing alignment lifts the arch, and helps with fallen arches, knee, and hip problems. However, sensing the distinction does impact self-imaging, which makes habit the master of control…thus making the process an overly detailed, overburdening sensitivity.

I took on more than I had realized at the time. I thought I was being practical, giving down-to-earth instructions. But control, knowing, and security are linked like an infant's delicate wrist bracelet worn even at night. Details, process, take time and unwittingly impede the flair of release that is so much a part of movement.

Just a few days ago, I saw a father lift a stroller with his little boy in it up the three steps to the flat area of the lobby of our building. The second they were on the flat surface, the little boy left the stroller, running down the hall like a rocket. The father caught up to him and carried him back to where I stood watching with delight. I looked at this sweet, blond-haired adventurer and said to him, "It's so much fun to run." He beamed a smile of approval for my putting words to what he felt. The union between us was palpable.

The perception of the 4th *toe alignment* is often clearer on one foot than the other. Achieving a symmetry of sensation over both feet requires each person to incrementally adjust the leg in which the 4th toe alignment feel least clear. This usually ends up in narrowing the distance between the legs. Exactly how much each person needs to narrow to sense a symmetrical 4th toe alignment varies. The person may also discover the need to inch one leg more forward to achieve a sensory symmetry through both legs. These adjustments are incremental, personal, combining sensation with perception, bringing mind and body together.

This level of sensitivity differs for each person. Emphasis on form and imitation unwittingly subordinates the individual's perceptual sensitivity.

Students also had to get used to tolerating each other's needs, as I dealt with the incremental adjustments for each person. Accommodating this group dynamic was a significant shift from the focus on keeping the energy of excitement in exercising. characteristic of my training that engenders group cohesion. *A fundamental aspect of mass zeal, of fascism, which I—nor I assume, did my instructors— considered at the time, or even now!*

I once had a control/power-savvy analyst who point-blank said, "Everything is politics." She had been the young Phi Beta Kappa lawyer who argued the acceptance or rejection of potential clients to the partners of a 250-year-old firm for a number of years before becoming a PhD psychologist/psychoanalyst. Her presentations won over the partners, following her convincing reasoning. "Never lost a case," she mentioned.

The 4th toe alignment process unconsciously helped me in the process of separation from bonding, as in my infant self from my mother. The ability to consciously adjust to symmetry was personally liberating. My circuitous, unwitting road to awareness continued!

The sensation rising from the 4th toe alignment heightened each person's focus on *sensing tactile motion*, in contrast to *just motion,* which is generally visualized by grasping what is wanted, wished for, and imagined. The tactile makes the visual, the anticipated aim physically real, texturally alive, generating a subtle, unwitting expression of feelings. The textural is specific, an extension of touch.

I was shifting from *just follow as best you can what I am demonstrating*, from describing into a more personal teaching. It slowed the driving energy of the class. I was taking too much time with individual corrections. That what I was showing and explaining applied to everyone didn't matter to some individuals. The distinction between movement and energy was a difficult emotional fusion to alter.

Sustaining the *4th toe alignment* while moving out into space became self-evident to me. It predicated *shortening* one's stride. Everyone needed to do so. This again slowed the sense of just "doing." I'll venture to speak of this unquestioned love of energy approach to exercises and dance in general, as masturbatory—self-excitation! Or, if everybody is doing it, it might be a kinder, more socially acceptable way to put it.

It took many years for me to understand this correlation between the outer and the inner as expressed on a physical level. It took much longer than I imagined.

These three practical considerations: 1) *Sense the 4th toe line,* 2) *Narrow Your Stance,* and 3) *Shorten Your Stride* help us stay more attuned to the *Motion* passing through muscles. This eventually became the premise of my book, *The Way of the 4th Toe.*

These simple adjustments have and can help *anyone, anywhere, at any time* they put them into practice. The 4th toe line creates an alive arch in the foot, making for a healthier, more sensed contact with the floor. It promotes the continuity of touch through the 40 muscles in each foot. This tactile sensation continues through the calf muscles. It alters our balance *ever* so slightly, lessening pressure on the heels. The *Motion* of that continuity is the essence of dance, of standing, of walking. The autonomic function of balance is brought into an awareness, allowing for a more conscious sense of muscular realigning, of unnoticed misalignments. We can affect posture dynamically in the process of standing, walking, and ultimately in the complexity of sport and the art of dance.

It slowly makes you aware of how *narrowing* your stance and subsequently *shortening* your stride facilitates a more fluid *Motion*, a greater sense of symmetry in our bilateral musculature. Embedded resistances, stiffening melts away instead of fighting with it. It allows the *motion* between muscles to function fluidly. Space and time open as an experience rather than as a wish. The struggle with our own body evaporates. Mind and body become one by this practice; it's not just a belief.

Patience is built into this perceptual practice. The mystery is unveiled by the practicality of the practice. It's all personal, not abstract. Time surrenders to the aliveness of your sensitivity. The master of control in us recognizes our perceptual awareness *of Motion*.

These three simple adjustments lessen stress on the joints as we stand and walk. They continually effect the *continuity of motion* through the muscles around the joints. The practice makes us aware that alignment is muscular, tactile, not just skeletal and postural. The *tactile perception* heightens the experience of *Motion* in movement. Over time, the perceptual attunement relaxes mind and body. This awareness of our working sensory system seamlessly facilitates the unconscious flow of feelings.

I assumed that the relationship of nerves to muscles was contributing to this startling emotional perception on my part. Nerve cells and muscle cells separate at the same time in the process of gestation,[42] impacting on each other throughout life; like identical twins, separate but uncannily close.

I was at first startled when I saw how this perceptual attention to the *Motion* from muscles to muscles happened; the somatically expressed feelings, not consciously thought! I didn't think of it then, but it's like a meditation on the breath that keeps us in the "Now," for want of a better way of referencing the effect of these simple adjustments.

The sensitivity to motion through the musculature corresponds, I conjectured, to the unconscious motion of feelings, The improvisor isn't conscious of thought *or* feelings, but those of us observing experience feelings emanating from the *Motion* of gestures and shapes. It is quite remarkable! It just happens!

The way it happens gives me the sense of getting closer to retrieving love.

Knowing, thinking, intellectualizing detracts from this sensitivity to *Motion.*

We love knowing. It makes us feel safe, in control. However, this sensory experience evokes a distinction between presence on a feeling level in contrast to presence on a knowing level. For those

---

42 During gastriculation in the third week, the embryo develops three layers—ectoderm, mesoderm, and endoderm—that differentiate into distinct tissues. The endoderm gives rise to neural tissue and the outer layer of skin. The mesoderm differentiates itself into skeletal and muscle tissue, blood and blood vessels. (See nursinghero.com)

of us who have experienced this distinction, we realize that they are not mutually exclusive; on the contrary. they feed each other creatively. Experiencing the feeling of what is being said or the silence between speaking is the essence of a sensitive relationship regardless of whatever engages us as individuals, be it friendship, creating, psychoanalysis, loving.

TACTILE CONTINUITY

My continuing focus on *tactile continuity* in the exercises was correcting misalignments that develop without us realizing what is happening in the process of growing up. These unnoticed misalignments eventually lead to coordination problems on a very practical level. And eventually to medical issues, back pain, joint issues, as well as to blockages in creative efforts, gestures disassociated from the togetherness of the whole body.

Although I was helping individuals with places of pain by suggesting alignment corrections, my focus was not medical. It remained movement-oriented, namely, what does the student need to become perceptually sensitive to facilitate a creative, heartfelt process of movement.

The fact of becoming more attuned to the subtlety of *motion* through the musculature resulted in a more organic flow from one movement to the next in their improvisation. Gestures and shapes germinated without intention, without aim, without self-consciousness. Feelings became apparent in both the silence and in the motion of every movement; and the compulsive, over-determined connection to movement loosened. At first, I called it *The Interplay of Muscles*.

The hardest part of this transition was psychological. The tendency was to think of improvisation as "letting go." Paying attention to sensing the contact of the feet rising from the ground as a tactile sensation of motion was difficult, and for some, burdensome. It was a departure from using movement to release tensions, repressed feelings. Our physical movement serves that purpose. When that purpose becomes habituated, "embodied," feelings are subdued by a somaticized defensive psychological mindset. Although movement as release feels liberating, the physicality becomes addictive, the skills become self-absorbing. The self-absorbing skill-focused movement helped me see how the release is so often a sequence of dissociated gestures kept together by imagination while avoiding the feeling experience. I could describe it as *acting out,* a more pathologic wording.

Could this unconscious avoidance of feelings be true of all art? Might this also be true of all creative thought, be it business or physics?

My personal therapy over the years played a role in my way of thinking about the freedom of movement. The element of *Motion* in movement became more central to creative movement. It provided a language to speak about why Jeffrey's *clay* that was so startlingly organic; he wasn't acting out. He was totally identifying with being a clump of clay. The *motion* from gestures into shapes was seamless.

It made clearer for me what the right focus for each developmental phase has to implicitly generate, *a Tactile Continuity of Motion.*

THE CONTINUITY OF MOTION: DETAILS, DETAILS, DETAILS

In dance, as in all movement, *The Continuity of Motion* should be the ultimate experiential integration of all techniques. I wish it would be. This has remained my definitive concept of what brings body and soul together. It's what I focus on with adults, what I want them to aim for.

The tactile is based on touch, the first and most primal sense in utero before all the other senses develop. By the eighth week of gestation, the touch receptors develop around the lips, face and nose, connecting to the brain. By the 12th week, the receptors form all over the body including, the genitals, palms, and soles of the feet. This specific textural sensing sensation must be nurtured slowly, because it is more vital to our brain development than sight, smell, or taste. For many years, I have started the exercises with the *contact* with the floor by the soles of our feet, consciously reinforcing the sensation of *contact*, the sustaining *touch* as the source of *motion* passing through the feet; and how flexing the knees effects a subtle body shift forward allowing the continuity of the tactile through the ankle and muscles of the calves.

As you can imagine, these subtle adjustments realign experientially the *continuity of motion*. The floor, the earth upon which we stand, enriches our relatedness, the continuation of the very fetal experience before coming out of the amniotic fluid, out of the waters and into the air. This process is addressed in many cultural concepts of evolution. It has been deeply understood by humans with different wordings since time immemorial.

Sustaining the textural *continuity of motion* dictates how it passes around joints to the adjoining muscles. It takes patience to sense the incremental torques that vary perceptually with each person. We call it "being in touch," as when a scent touches us, or a taste or a color. We are connecting emotionally, personally.

Continuity in movement is too often a self-observing process, like looking at ourselves in the mirror. The self-observing is split off from the self-experience that literally keeps us in touch. Although they are mutually inclusive, the splitting by the visual rationalized as "reality" is a mentalized sense of relatedness.

Although movement takes place through muscles, the visual imaging often supersedes the actual tactile continuity. Naming what we are doing becomes more central than the feeling. We look at ourselves more than we remain sensitive to the specifics of what is happening on a kinesthetic level. *Intent overshadows feeling*. Mind over matter. The pride of knowing is a pretty common developmental problem. Keeping these mental views of ourselves as connected makes for feelings always to be sensed along with how we word them.

Self-distancing from the tactile process predicated incremental self-perceptions of the textural motion, moving through muscles around joints. An example is the perception of the fingertips moving through the back of the hand with a small torque passing over the inside of ring finger, then over the outside of the forearm muscles, then around the outer top of the elbow for the *line* to be sensed through the upper arm musculature passing over the shoulder joint into the upper back,

114

neck, and down the back. This level of perception—I repeat—requires patience. This was in contrast to moving from joint to joint, fingertips to armpit, which is a skeletal self-imaging, more easily remembered by young children for whom need/ wish/desire most often dictates their relatedness. The metaphor of freedom for grownups is expansive and potentially domineering, engendering a compulsive aggression. *Violence is a consequence of impatience.*

We all need empathic mothering, along with care. I think the idiom *haste makes waste* says it well.

Sensing muscular *tactile* alignment is a sensitivity that has to be reestablished anew each time, in the present. It eventually makes sensing the pads of the toes on both feet helpful. The awareness of the pads of the toes registered as significant only in my 80s, when a male student returned to class after a hospital stay with a lung and breathing problem. Aware of his tendency to throw himself into "his feeling of the music" (his words) with abandon, I suggested sensing the pads of his toes as he moved into space. I had referenced the imagined 4*th* *toe line* in the past, but this was different; by sensing the touch of the pads with the ground as a starting sensation, the togetherness with which his motion altered was startling! I asked everyone to sense the pads of their toes that, like osmosis, made everyone's movement comparably more cohesive.

The tactile progression through the legs rising into the musculature under the buttocks is my way of understanding this phenomenon of wholeness. It was clearly in contrast to a first position ballet placement, tightening muscles that, not uncommonly, result in problems.

A personal note: I disliked my parents' crooked, misshapen toes and the way my own toes appeared to me. I marvel to consider how this childhood judgment denied a part of my body for so many years! Denial, rejection, dismissiveness stare us in the face in moments of unbearable feelings about ourselves or about life itself. A part of the body can become an obsession, a literal representation of the hidden inner self, a totem.

Spreading the toes helps us to sense the pad of each toe more specifically. In doing so, you can sense how the body shifts slightly forward, lessening the bearing down pressure on the heels, which in turn relaxes the lower back that develops unconsciously to counterbalance the stiffening of the legs. This is what ballet positioning tries to deal with by the rotation of the upper back of thighs into the buttocks in the plié, to affect a *continuity of form* between legs and torso.

Discovering how to affect this unity through the torques in the musculature facilitates a more tactile flow, more variations in muscle tonus, a more emotionally alive continuity. The most emotionally talented dancers actuate this connectedness: Mikhail Baryshnikov, Carmen de Lavallade, and Suzanne Farrell, to name the few whom I have witnessed as having this tactile sensitivity, regardless of how they personally may have thought of it. There is no question in my mind at present that it references the feeling flow in the person. I used to refer to the variations as qualities, like Laban: heavy, hard, light, soft. Or the reader may be more familiar with how a person speaks, how the speech is modulated; more expressive of feelings.

This subtle shift in balance lightens the sense of the whole body. Strikingly, it made *every* one of my students aware that balance is not totally determined autonomically. We can affect the unconscious compensatory balancing process that doesn't ask for our permission. The description is much lengthier than how easily we can make these subtle changes. Flexing the knees helps, because you no longer must stiffen the knees for strength, i.e. support. The support, the balance is affected by the *continuity of motion*. One can sense how this adjustment, like a wave, moves throughout the whole body. It's akin to the quantum physics wave theory of energy no longer boxed-in as a solid form. The more adventurous contemporary architecture deals with these aesthetic issues as well.

Baryshnikov, whom I recently encountered sitting one seat away from me at a dance concert, comes to mind. I don't know whether he thought or thinks about the tactile *continuity of motion,* but his emotional sensibility was demonstrated during a performance of his I attended at the Brooklyn Academy of Music, through a very delicate gesture with a simple finger, a wrist motion as he turned his back to the audience, as if his heart spoke while walking behind Willem Dafoe, an exquisite physical actor, but not in my perception equal to Baryshnikov's muscular finesse.[43] He responded to my recollection with a smile, adding, "I spoke to Dafoe, but it didn't register." He made a point of shaking my hand when he stood. I don't know what he was thinking, but I considered the handshake as the joining of our hearts through touch.

I'm defining freedom as a softening of an unconsciously held belief, habit, or pattern. In this case, it is the emotional result of alignment that happens by sensing the pads of our toes, which no longer have to curl-in like the claws of a bird holding onto branches. The window of freedom is opened by the minutia of Details.

Such sensitive placement will vary from one person to the next. It is very personal, very individual, albeit theoretically the same for everyone. Only adults can perceptually affect such incremental adjustments. It tests our patience, the delicate discrimination of sensation. The quickness of visually imaging is brought down to earth by the tactile sensation. Our sense of time is challenged. Our sense of

---

43 The 2014 Robert Wilson production I attended at the Brooklyn Academy of Music (BAM) of *The Old Woman,* by avant-garde absurdist writer Daniil Kharms, was developed with Baryshnikov.

the whole body, of *form,* is challenged. Physical feeling and emotional feeling meet by virtue of the specificity of alignment. *Our feelings flow through the non-resistant body.* The abstraction of feelings miraculously disappears. The mind relaxes.

Once I became aware of this dimension of sensitivity, which I used to call talent—magically endowed like God's breath that made the clay of Adam alive—I was able to articulate it in practical, physical terms. This process is available to all of us.

An earlier approach to this awareness was preceded by forming a class in 1975 that was based on exploring the inner feeling of space, which, as you'll recall, I first experienced with Aryeh Kalev using the concentration technique. I called it *Inner Space.*

INNER SPACE:
A SENSORY EXPERIENCE
OF SPACE

Inner Space began as a two-hour class for advanced students who had been working with me for a good number of years. I thought of it as an exploration of Ego Relationships. I thought at the time how a sensitivity to the *inner space* experience with Aryeh Kalev had altered my concrete, circumscribed experience of space. The class was structured, like most classes, by exercises, followed by the concentration technique.

Movement was slowed down into *motion,* and *motion experienced as muscular tactile continuity.* The centering contact of the back of the head to the ground was sustained through the imaged lines for a good hour.

When the students stood, relaxed, breathing quietly, sensing arms longer and toes further away than usual, they walked around the studio a few times before I introduced music for improvisation. I was using the sustaining function of memory of their sensory awakening for the *inner sensation of motion.*

After repeating this initial imagining process for a number of sessions to reinforce the inner sensory awakening of the body, I looked to see whether this inner sense of motion was sustained in their improvisations. Observing how sections of the body were not fully engaged evoked exploring three other centers: *chest (high) center*, *torso front (middle) center*, and *pelvis (low) center*. These four centers were my physical approach to help them sense the whole body, to stimulate a more emotionally sensitive spatial experience.

These centers corresponded to my training in a variety of dance techniques. After establishing each one with improvisations to music to support their integration, we would sit in a circle as each person shared their experience. Allocating time for the verbal exchange introduced a more therapeutic element to the group.

To deal with my perception that each center needed to be more fully experienced, I explored the *front* of the head center, then the *back* of the head center. I did this with all the centers, chest, middle, and pelvic centers. And eventually the *hollow middle* of each center, akin to air flowing through the torso, like God's breath into the clay of Adam. As always, I combined front, middle, and back with each center.

Sensing each center as distinct felt new, imaginative, intellectually stimulating. Combining these distinct perceptual explorations was a whole-body mind experience, feeding their imaginative, intellectual sensibilities. They visualized each center in a discreet, contrasting way that pleased them.

It is emphatically clear to me, in hindsight, that the adding of front, back, and hollow middle suggests something missing in my emotional perception that needed filling, like an empty wine glass at the dinner table. I kept trying to stimulate a wholeness that I failed to sense when observing individual and group improvisatory interactions. I could easily equate gestures, shapes, and movement sequences into a story line, but continued to sense a generalized, habituated improvisational language by each one of these gifted and celebrated individuals as lacking in a tactile expression of feeling.

I now have the professional language to consider my failure to sense the emotional investment in their improvisations as possibly my projection; putting onto them what I was not feeling in myself, my own weary, impaired capacity to love. But maybe both perceptions were true?

I felt pedagogically secure finding a creative movement approach to *Space* that was different from *Directions*. What remained regarding my conceptual model was a way to do the same thing with *Time*.

INNER TIME:

The Sensory of Experience of Time

Since I had already associated *Head Center* with a ceremonial carriage—the miter headdress of bishops, the crown of queens, the veil of brides—Gregorian music was a fitting soundtrack. It became quite obvious that each center prompted a change in breathing. *Head Center* generated an inhalation sensed through the top of the nostrils passing up the front of the forehead, top of the head, down the back of the neck, and spine into the lungs, as in a deeply relaxed sleep cycle.

The *Chest High Center* is the more familiar front/middle nostril inhalation moving into the back of the throat, descending through the thorax, filling the lungs, exhaling through the nose or mouth; a more conscious kind of breathing while walking, or other activities that involve effort, not physically taxing.

The *Middle Torso Center* breath is associated with more physically demanding activities, resulting in open mouth breathing-in-and-out, to keep up with the demands of the activity requiring endurance, corresponding to an underlying anxiety about finishing or winning as in sports. It was more easily explored with music asking for speed or physical excitement, like Afro-Cuban drums or hot jazz, which accentuated a more driven self-experience.

The fourth breathing exploration was dictated by an emotionally overdetermined energy. I associated it with Martha Graham's *contraction/release,* a gut sensation that needs—demands—release. Imagine a gut-wrenching fear struggling for air, exploding into a cry. Graham gravitated to Greek mythology as a story frame to contain this powerful force that drove her. Inhalation and exhalation were governed by this emotional physical sensibility. The explosive quality of Impulsivity characterizes the dramatic gestures/shapes of emotions. The connection between one movement and the next is characterized by a sudden freezing and then release, because the subtlety of feeling is cut by the sharp holding back of the contraction. We are being invited and pushed away at the same time.

Graham's choreography was dramatically exciting. She eventually developed a terrible arthritis, a form of conversion hysteria, a paralysis of unfathomable rage. She created some memorable dances, revealing her personal story, about our human, emotional, and psychic encounters.

The fifth pelvic center is breathing, generated by the body with no obvious connection to inhaling/exhaling. Tight, jazzy, now rock, non-stop movement, keep going with no consideration for breathing. Exciting, driven movement, impressive, relentless.

Five breathing explorations. Each one, as in the *Centers* explorations, eliciting a distinct sensory experience evoking its *own Inner Time.*

The accompanying music went from angelic, Gregorian chants to love ballads, like Charlie Chaplin's words and music creation of "Smile," as sung memorably by Nat King Cole...followed by the seductive jazz counterpoint of *"Take Five"* by Dave Brubeck. There is a lot of music that can accompany these breathing patterns.

Fixated breathing patterns, symptomatic of excessive control, impacts our lives, our likes and dislikes, our speech patterns, our thought patterns, diminishing our capacity for change and adaptation that life and relationships uninvitingly bring to our awareness. These time explorations were my effort to bring embedded, unconscious patterns into awareness, in the hope of eliciting a physically fuller, emotional resonance, such as that which I first felt back in 1959 while watching Jeffrey perform his *clay* improvisation.

This was my last attempt to deal with the curricular format I had framed as true of all dance techniques, starting with the children classes in 1959.

For those readers who have been following the psychological aim of these explorations, it might suggest a pedagogic displacement of going back in time to infancy, when all we have is a sensory system that responds to whatever presents itself; sensory memory without a context. I sublimated through my teaching in a creatively engrossing way to reengage the early experiences we all have, before our caretaker becomes the discreet object we call mother, and long before we call it love. It never fully worked for me, albeit metaphorically, poetically, with a promise of a pot of fame at the end of the rainbow.

The class lasted for 17 years, dissolving in 1992, with a group of celebrated scholars, artists, and dancers crediting me over the years with inspirations for their work and celebrated publications.

As much as I enjoyed their praise, my heart wasn't touched. I wanted something that perhaps was unfair to their discoveries and pleasure. Then again, perhaps not?

ENDINGS

With the end of my second lease at 20 West 20th Street—where I at first created two studios, a massage space, and a therapy office on the tenth floor for the first five years, and then moved to the fifth floor to create a studio, dressing spaces, and an office area, while maintaining the massage and therapy space on the tenth floor for another five years—my wife and I separated after 24 years, and legally divorced as agreed a year later.

A low-grade anxiety of uncertainty hovered over me thereafter. I decided to leave the burgeoning Chelsea area at the end of the second five-year lease, returning the adult classes to the West Side. The one exception was prompted by the parents of my Saturday children's classes, who pleaded with me to continue. I found a studio just a block away on Fifth Avenue. After two years, I stopped giving the children's classes, and I ended the School for Creative Movement as an entity after 30 years. This was another emotionally unsettling experience; the children's program was the reason I started the School for Creative Movement.

Low-grade anxiety deepened into a life of aloneness. The excitement of growth, of self-importance, of belonging that had kept aloneness at bay, became undeniable. Unexpectedly, a French woman taking class with another teacher during the last year of the tenth-floor lease asked me for a copy of the *Creative Movement for the Classroom* book to give to a therapist she had worked with in

Paris who was thinking of starting a children's program. Hesitantly, attraction flowered enough for love to find me. By the second year of courting her and traveling to France to meet her parents, I surprised her father with my old-fashioned request for his daughter's hand. We married later that year, reawakening a deeper private life as a couple.

The Continuity of Motion was becoming increasingly irrefutable to me as the sensory experience to be pursued with adult students. Entering a second marriage revived my sense of continuity, personally and pedagogically.

SENSITIVITY REVIVED

Sensing the pads of the toes was added to the *4th toe alignment,* ensuring a more specific tactile sensation for the beginning of the exercises. This simple addition affected the placement of each person's stance with subtle, incremental adjustment to effect symmetry in the feet and legs, keeping alive the *tactile continuity.* The pads of toes accentuated the 4th toe line through the sole of each foot, and in turn affected another subtle shift of balance over the center of the feet, with a slight flexing of the knees, allowing for a clearer perception of *tactile motion* through the calf muscles.

As this alignment is sensed, so too is the awareness of the gracilis muscle, a long muscle rising from the inner part of the knee joint into the connecting tissue of the pubis and the upper half of pubic arch, which strengthened the connection of the legs to the pelvis, engaging the lower abdominals just above the pubis. The legs and torso begin to work and feel connected. *A significant change of awareness, contrasting the usual rotation of the thigh muscles into the buttocks, as in the ballet positions.*

Paying attention to the gracilis muscle automatically relaxes the lumbar vertebrae, eliminating the over-accentuated lower back curvature which unconsciously develops to counterbalance the stiffening of the legs. This common development is why the torso and arms are so dominant for most people to express feelings.

From my perspective, the unwitting, unconscious separation of torso and arms from legs is a dissociative development, emphasizing shape, form, and metaphor rather than the sensory tactile experience. Most people have no idea why this happens; they just like the freedom of torso and arms. This takes them away from what they are emotionally sensing. They believe the freedom of just moving is emotionally liberating, and are unconscious of the splitting off of their own sensory experience from that sense of freedom, just as meaning, words can displace the sensory tactile experience.

The tactile connection through the whole body is what differentiated Baryshnikov for me from other dancers. Others referred to it as his talent. He has been honored worldwide with a myriad of awards and accolades for his physically palpable, emotional communication. I suspect that Baryshnikov did not think of his connectedness in my terms. Perhaps it was the fluidity of his feelings that drove his acting explorations.

Again: *patience* is necessary for the perceptual awareness of subtle, individual adjustments of tactile motion. *It changes the not-uncommon compulsive physical action, transmuting it into feelings.*

When I first wrote about the garcilis, I conveniently skipped over the emotional transition from the explicit freedom of cognitive choices and meanings to the more limiting, potentially claustrophobic experience of *tactile continuity*; the sense of feeling stuck in the body. I have painfully lived through this conflict. I can assure you that it was not easy for me. I needed help to accommodate and integrate language, memory, and choices, so dominant in my development during toddlerhood, with the complexity of approaching adulthood.

How the tactile specificity is carried over into the improvisation is personal. Some parts of the *continuity of motion* are sustained,

130

while other parts are unwittingly disavowed by the dancer's personal movement habits.

In light of this last statement of mind over body, you can appreciate the many personal conflict and resistances that arise and must be respected and dealt with thoughtfully. These are not issues that can be thought of as "I am right, and you are wrong." Habits develop slowly and are intimately connected to our primal relationships in both conscious and unconscious ways. We can easily lose our core- self in accommodating another. The *Continuity of Motion* was a process of reclaiming a self-core experience.

The compulsion to act has several names: intuition, impulses, choices, following the music...all of which subordinate the perceptual sensory experience of tactile motion, often stated as, "I'm just following my feelings." Choices, desire, wanting, are not feelings. They can easily mask sadness, loneliness, unresolved pain going back to infancy, when you might have been cared for and admired, but not empathically sensed; which, as the British psychoanalyst D. W. Winnicott[44] pointed out, is the source of emotional security.

---

44 *The Capacity To Be Alone. 1958: International Journal of Psychoanalysis, 39:416-420.*

TERROR:

COVID, Short Then Long

My initial reaction to abdominal discomfort was to think of anxiety. When it didn't subside, my second call to the internist was responded to with "Go directly to emergency."

On March 26, 2020, I was taken by ambulance to the hospital and put into Stall 18 with an intravenous fluid tube, where I fell asleep. I was totally out of it while the labs did what they needed to do to determine what I was suffering with.

I awoke shocked by my feces-filled underpants, dislodged by my body with no inkling of what was happening while I slept. A deeply-embedded automatic alert system had been shockingly suspended. I experienced a sense of shame, of urgency, breathlessly communicated by cell phone to my wife: "Please bring me another pair of underpants as soon as you can."

The underwear was delivered to the information counter; no one was allowed past that curved marble counter. It was the beginning of the COVID-19 pandemic that claimed an extraordinary number of lives in short order. My very adult daughter in California subsequently told me, after I was out of the hospital, "We didn't expect you to come out alive." I was 86. People my age were being taken in increasing number by the zealously awaiting angel of death.

The morning of the 27th, a much younger male was wheeled into Stall 18. I was told, "We are moving you to the 10th floor into a private room." In the process, I left my black cashmere winter coat draped over the back of a chair, along with my cell phone, charger, and my glasses, with no sense of having left anything behind.

I was childishly excited by "a private room."

A female doctor came to see me on the afternoon of March 28th. I was again excited, focusing on her looks, orienting myself by my well-worn seductive lens, as if this was the beginning of a tryst.

"How do you feel?" she asked.

"I feel good," I answered. "When can I go home?"

"Maybe tomorrow. Let's see."

She left, and came back the following morning to release me from the hospital. I was wheeled down to the information counter in the lobby to see my beautiful wife getting a little bit more information. I reacted impatiently. "Where is the cab? Let's go."

Some days after returning home, she told me, "I was shocked when I saw you wheeled down. You were not the same Jack I know. When I looked into your eyes, there was nobody there!"

I didn't know what she was talking about. I felt fine, like my old self. March 29th, 2020. Three days. *That was quick! Denial is quick.*

The disparity in our perception of each other made the shell enveloping our relationship more transparent. She remained increasingly attentive to my fragility as I continued my delusional patterns of seductive assumptions and being in control.

By the second week back at home, I received a phone call from a follow-up nurse, who told me, "You are no longer contagious."

Whatever it was that had allowed me to sleep was wearing off. I couldn't stay in bed at night, rising to write page after page of thoughts that I always treated as "this has always helped me," with a sense of, *I know what is happening.* I was in and out of bed constantly, disturbing my wife's sleep. Out of concern for my strange, disturbed behavior, she kept to herself. I returned to bed at two, three, four o'clock in the morning, and then two sleepless episodes awake to meet the morning light. During one of those nights, as I lay on the couch exhausted, I couldn't move the fingertips of my right hand; followed by seeing myself sitting behind the stirring wheel at a STOP sign with the option to move but unable to decide whether to turn right or left. I was frighteningly confused, trembling with disorientation. The fear was stronger than my cognitive resources.

I called a recommended psychoanalyst for help the following day. The analyst listened attentively to the details of my couch story. I could hear myself talking to him as if I were totally in control of my senses. I was a peer psychoanalyst, a published author, a renowned creative movement expert. Why was I trying to impress him with how worthy I was for him as a patient, when I was so unbelievably desperate?

I was incapable of distinguishing circumstance from feeling. I described what I sensed, as if it would be totally clear to the listener what I felt; the way a toddler assumes others understand by virtue of their description. This assumption continues with many adults into old age.

I was physically exhausted, in a manic state. The first thing the analyst said to me that triggered my recovery was, "There was nobody there for you when you were learning to move your fingertips."

His comment was at first interesting, but disconnected from the fear coursing through every part of me, it began to pull me out of my terror. I was so desperate for help that I submitted to it, as I did when I was in the emergency stall in the hospital.

"There was nobody there..." The words conjured up my mother from the grave I kept her in. She became present. I wasn't terrifyingly alone! The solitary darkness was lit by *there was nobody there.*

Overwhelming anxiety began to counterbalance my overactive thinking. A low-dosage medication prescribed by a psychiatrist helped me sleep. I was exhausted. I needed to sleep. The writing pads were put aside. I had entered the universe of sensory emanations; I had so avidly pursued this pedagogically as a creative movement teacher, but couldn't distinguish these sensory emanations from feeling. It pains me to acknowledge how out of touch I was with feeling.

The dependency on my analyst was a blessing of relief. I was grateful that there was someone there for me. Shame was unraveling. The spotlight on my self-importance was dimming.

The ensuing therapy sessions brought up more details of how "she" wasn't there for me. The child in me began to breathe by blaming the resurrected mother. I assumed that the analyst's comment had to do with her absence. The analyst in me realized how I had swallowed her impatience along with her colostrum. My *impatience* showed up in a lifetime of eating too fast, while others were still savoring their food. Impatience gestated emotionally well into my 80s and throughout more than 60 years of creative work. The mother lived inside of me, a forever attachment that cannot wither, no matter how I claimed a separate self. Anxiety was relegated to the anticipation of night, when angels and devils visit as disguised dreams, testifying to the inescapable truth of the dreams and fantasies that live in us.

Solutions to these private dramas don't have to be immediate. The analytic process in all its guises is not surgery. The constancy of her anxiety gestating through my tiny cells was usually unbearable. I had been not just abandoned, but terrified by her emotional sadness. I began to vibrate unwanted sensations without respite. The depressed infant/me started shedding dried-up tears, as the arrogance of thought bowed its head to the sensory vibrations.

My father awakened out of my judgmental disregards, swayed by my mother's anger with him. She never understood his self-protection against the fear, depression, and repressed rage over the abandonments he suffered, which he camouflaged with humor to defend against his aloneness at age 11, when his mother died. His father returned and left again. His wife—my mother—loved his tenderness, but believed that she was the rightful substitute for his emptiness.

My father, who walked through Warsaw dodging bullets to see her, never quite seemed to get beyond my mother's anxiety and projections about his inadequacy. Since he could not fully acknowledge the depth of his terrifying fears, he did not realize how terrified she was. They lived liberated from traditional orthodoxy as Jewish socialists, embracing their Jewishness, their *yiddishkeit*, the language, friendships, laughter, and hard work, to hide their lonely wandering selves.

I had unconsciously invented separate thrones for each of my parents in my storyline palace; an awareness for the child/me to survive the acknowledgment of them as a couple before I presumed to be a part of the triad. Three-plus Covid years passed, unveiling my virginal self. As Freud put it, analysis interminable.[45]

The transference to my analyst became unequivocal. He was my Wizard of Oz, listening to the center of my brain, giving me a heart, emboldening my courage, loosening my skeletal tensions. During one of my early sessions while speaking about my mother my voice involuntarily rose into a shout, "I love my mother." I shocked myself. I was no longer unquestioningly in control. Something ancient was rising from the ashes—a self that lived outside of the boundaries of time. I was opening up to feelings about my past that were intellectually exciting but emotionally alarming, as feelings became

---

45 Freud's monograph on "Analysis Terminable and Interminable." 1937: SE.

more dominant than the delusions that helped me survive petrifying fears. Fears expressed symptomatically: needing more air in the room, an unsettled stomach, stiffened muscles, trembling nerves, fear of death, breakdown, madness, as Winnicott illuminated.[46]

The emotional sense of death didn't happen until I was in my 91st year, when I sensed my whole torso drop through my pelvic floor, scaring the hell out of me with a forever abandonment; like a baby whose mother stepped away for far too many seconds, as infant research videos show. I couldn't believe my emotional falling.

Processing my survival involved repeated calls for sessions, walking with a woozy physical and emotional sense of imbalance for a couple of years, persistent thoughts of aging. My skin thinning, reacting to any bump or scrape with breaking capillary blood spots that no longer healed quickly. Needing to speak, too often, to my wife: "Listen, please listen." I was a pain, in unfathomable never-before emotional pain! Was I speaking to my wife, my mother, my dad, my children, my peers, the world, God? The emptiness of poverty, of loneliness, emanating crazy sounds or gibberish, were all a part of surviving the buried self, asking to be acknowledged.

Adults have the experience, the capacity to survive the infant/toddler/child that could only get sick, hide, run away, make up stories, play in denial, and not uncommonly, in arrogant cynicism.

After Covid, the rage, the cry finally broke through for atonement, to apologize for the hurt I had caused while in pain. I had long hidden in my body and danced, choreographed, directed theater, was featured in *The New York Times Sunday Magazine*, published, became a psychoanalyst, thought endlessly, and finally began, like the multitudes

---

46 Winnicott, Donald W. "Fear of Breakdown." 1974: *International Review of Psychoanalysis*, 1:103-107.

of people working, surviving with unresolved issues appearing like ghosts, speaking with a tremor, unshed sensed tears, a constantly warm upper back, somatic moments that would demand to be improvised in movement because they were unable to be acknowledged in any other way. Fortunately, the overwhelming terror that engendered silence can now at least be described to share with you, the reader.

As the tormented pain dissipated, my physical balance slowly returned. The infantile past continued to appear. Pandora's box had been opened and could not be closed. The calls to the analyst diminished. I have never returned to a former self-seducing delusional self, nor do I want to.

My mother spoke to me about *gedult,* patience. A mother when I was under the age of three would still embrace me on her knees and sing me to sleep: *Shluf mine Yankele, farmach dee oigen.* That little boy recently stood beside me to speak and be spoken to. "I hear you. I won't abandon you. I promise. I'm tired, would you help me sleep? This old man needs to sleep. You can stay next to me. OK?"

It sounds totally hallucinatory, but I felt his presence. The little boy and the old man were holding hands as surely as day follows night. I had never had such a hallucinatory experience. The former me would have thought *you're mad to live in that world of Totems, personified animals, living rocks, plants, teddy bears, which I never had.* In fact, I never had any toys, we were too poor. How does one share the presence of early, early life without reverting to speaking of it in the past tense, to sound rational in the present? I can sense the swelling of tears in my eyes as I read my confession.

More recently, I broke into uncontrollable sobbing tears for the last 15 minutes of a session, and again for another hour, sobbing to my wife to convey as best as I could what I had experienced in those last

15 minutes, bidding my mother, dead since 1980, to go in health to her death. *A living separation, a long time coming.*

I tried doing the same for my father, just to be fair, but I sensed that it wasn't real. There was more processing to do. His capacity to deny and project was closer to my sublimations asking for a deeper quieter compassion for him and myself. It took another year of unbearable silence to separate from his gift of play and humor.

Dealing with time by the sensed difference of the five distinct breathing patterns— which I have detailed in an earlier section— is pedagogic, lacking in the living experience of one's emotional presence, one's coexistence with the living self that is not memory, not a mirror, not a looking glass, not a meditation. It is perhaps the essence of empathy, of relatedness out of aloneness.

ATTUNEMENT

A surprising, intuitive poem I wrote on 9/21 while still recovering from Covid and continuing my analytic sessions might be appropriate at this juncture:

Love is an experience.
It happens and yet you didn't feel it coming.
It covers your whole being as a breath that you did not inhale.
It appears without a mirror.
You remember, but you cannot possess it, nor repeat it, no matter
how quickly you shape it.
Love lives, but you did not create it.

What happened to me was undeniable. It is simply human love, which we do not control. Moments of loneliness intermittently continue to descend like the fog of a hovering cloud, disappearing with the morning rays from the center of my inner galaxy. The unspoken chants, the unheard whispers, the untouched quivers, the unseen glints continually resonate. When I lie down to sleep, unwished-for thoughts appear that have no aim, go nowhere. Thinking as if fear has a solution when there is nothing to fear. I do not want to feel pain, ever. The absolute sound of "ever" evokes the infant's extreme experiences. No modulations. Being and nothingness, alive and dead, endless infinity before God, the omnipotent. Feelings freed from the boundaries of circumstance. It's just us beings, being!

Attunement, like all character changes, happens; its time is uncontrollable to become a lived-in way of living. Accepted without choice. Humility without choice. Experiencing without choice.

Just this morning, a second dream laid to rest an earlier confusing dream, opening my eyes with a deep, deep calm. I felt as if had awakened from a sealed envelope at 90, on the cusp of 91. It's all private, irrefutably personal, cannot be copied. It is just me. It is just you.

THE PRESENT

I no longer look at movement from a purely alignment perspective, regardless of the legitimacy of physically grounding the person. Improvisations as an extension of the child's pride—*I can walk, I can run, I can jump, I can imagine*—now appear as acts of daring escapes when gestures and shapes suggest fear, anger, sadness, loss, loneliness, relatedness.

The universe we're born into has seconds, minutes of terror, sadness, delight not of our making. If those terrifying seconds and minutes come and go, do we recover and speak of unconditional love, of pride in our skills...do we live in safety, pray with kindness, I wonder?

How does one convey these very personal, often anonymous, unspoken feelings, while teaching, when engaging patients, and, most sensitively, to one's wife, children, friends, whom we treat with expectations of intimacy?

While teaching, I continued to focus on the alignment work during the exercise part of the class with a greater emphasis on how each incremental, personal adjustment contributes to the *continuity of motion* as the ultimate awareness of both exercising, improvisation, life. I take more time for us to observe and respond to an individual's improvisational increments of motion emerging unencumbered by aim, purpose, intent, or reason. They are totally immersed in the experience of motion, dancing, not reflecting. It is amazing how often the improvisor did not— does not—register feeling associations. Reactions are shaped by questions. "It felt different, it felt good" is often the response. There is a calm as though conflicts have vanished, regardless of the gestures and shapes suggesting otherwise. We share our feelings, our thoughts to the improvisor. When it corresponds to what they felt but had not put into words, the person feels embraced. The body expressing feelings not named, feelings not intended, physical associations without judgement: this is truly creative dance… as my heart had wished for, but was unable to verbalize for so long beyond *something is missing*.

The work with patients became quieter, with longer listening segments empathically alive for both the patient and me. Fewer closures, as the underlying emotional experience for the patient became more evident and tolerable. The walls of anxiety crumbling by the sound of trumpets bellowing irrepressible feelings. This was analysis, Freudian archeology, revealing hidden truths, ego supplanting id, significant objects of early life incarnated, a space of vitality between patient and therapist evolving as love.

At long last I feel my wife's care and fears, the love of patients regardless of how they might think of it, the love of students who listen appreciatively to my observations and suggestions, the love of my adult children who are happy I am alive to their love…a love lost, now found.

www.ingramcontent.com/pod-product-compliance
Lightning Source LLC
Chambersburg PA
CBHW071406120626
46546CB00002B/840